FIXING AND FLIPPING REAL ESTATE

STRATEGIES FOR THE POST-BOOM ERA

Marty Boardman

Apress®

ISBN-13 (pbk): 978-1-4302-4644-2
ISBN-13 (electronic): 978-1-4302-4645-9

President and Publisher: Paul Manning
Acquisitions Editor: Jeff Olson
Editorial Board: Steve Anglin, Mark Beckner, Ewan Buckingham, Gary Cornell, Louise Corrigan, Morgan Ertel, Jonathan Gennick, Jonathan Hassell, Robert Hutchinson, Michelle Lowman, James Markham, Matthew Moodie, Jeff Olson, Jeffrey Pepper, Douglas Pundick, Ben Renow-Clarke, Dominic Shakeshaft, Gwenan Spearing, Matt Wade, Tom Welsh
Coordinating Editor: Rita Fernando
Copy Editor: Joanna Meekins
Compositor: Bytheway Publishing Services
Indexer: SPi Global
Cover Designer: Anna Ishchenko

Distributed to the book trade worldwide by Springer Science + Business Media New York, 233 Spring Street, 6th Floor, New York, NY 10013. Phone 1-800-SPRINGER, fax (201) 348-4505, e-mail orders-ny@springer-sbm.com, or visit www.springeronline.com. Apress Media, LLC is a California LLC and the sole member (owner) is Springer Science + Business Media Finance Inc (SSBM Finance Inc). SSBM Finance Inc. is a **Delaware** corporation.

For information on translations, please e-mail rights@apress.com or visit www.apress.com.

Apress and friends of ED books may be purchased in bulk for academic, corporate, or promotional use. eBook versions and licenses are also available for most titles. For more information, reference our Special Bulk Sales–eBook Licensing web page at www.apress.com/bulk-sales.
Any source code or other supplementary materials referenced by the author in this text is available to readers at www.apress.com. For detailed information about how to locate your book's source code, go to www.apress.com/source-code/.

This is book is dedicated to my daughters, Allyson and Audrey. They inspire me every day with their intelligence, creativity, and beauty. My hope is they grow up understanding that with proper effort, dedication, decisiveness, humility, and optimisim, they can achieve their goals. I also want them to know that it's okay to fail, as long as they fail forward. It's how we all learn and grow. I love you, girls.

Contents

About the Author

Marty Boardman is the owner and chief financial officer of Rising Sun Capital Group, LLC, a private real estate investment firm in Gilbert, Arizona. His company fixes and flips houses throughout the greater Phoenix metro housing market. He's been the principal in over 250 single-family residential real estate transactions since 2002, and in more than 80 since the housing market crash of 2008. Marty is also an accredited instructor for the Arizona Department of Real Estate and a national contributor to BiggerPockets.com, an online real estate investment magazine. His real estate investing articles have been published on AOL Real Estate and Realtor.com. He is a presenter at conferences devoted to real estate investment. He blogs at flippingphoenixhouses.com.

Acknowledgments

My wife, Linda, was three months pregnant with my first daughter when I quit my job in television news in 2002 to start investing in real estate. She continued to work a full-time job while I stayed at home with our first-born baby girl.

I worked evenings and weekends and earned $24,000 the first year. She accepted the role as primary breadwinner for the family with patience and grace. When my business began firing on all cylinders in 2004, she left the workforce to take care of my oldest daughter, Allyson, and our newborn baby Audrey, so I could focus on growing our company. When the crash came in 2008, she went back to work to help make ends meet.

Through all of the ups and downs Linda never lost faith in me or demanded that I go find a real job. After 14 years of marriage, I love and appreciate her now more than ever. Thank you, Linda, for allowing me to pursue my dream through triumph and failure.

To Keith, thank you for helping me get back on my feet in 2009 and teaching me the four-boxes concept for fixing and flipping real estate. You are my mentor, friend, and brother in Christ.

To Manny Romero, thanks for being the best business partner a guy could ever have (and for constantly reminding me to be a better listener). Your patience and perspective are a blessing.

To my mom and dad, Jim and Brenda Boardman, thank you for making me believe that I could do whatever I wanted in this world and for always supporting me, through the good and bad. Mom, I cherish our regular chats on the phone about the girls, food, sports, and techno gadgets. Dad, I couldn't have written this book without including some of your most famous quotes.

To my brother, Curtis, you are my best friend. Thanks for all your unique insight on life and the laughs.

To my mother and father-in-law, Richard and Martha Siegmund, thank you for raising an amazing woman and for accepting me into the family. I'm humbled by your love and generosity.

To my editor, Jeff Olson, thanks for finding me in cyberspace and giving me the opportunity to write this book. I appreciate your patience and the calm, subtle nudging it took to get this thing finished.

To the gang at Bergies Coffee in downtown Gilbert, Arizona, including Brian, Bruce, Christina, and Linda—many thanks for letting me hang out at the corner hightop table, tapping away on my laptop. There were many days when the only thing that could get me out of bed was the aroma and flavor of your special roast of the day.

And last, but certainly not least, glory to God for the gifts I've received. I'm honored by Your grace and grateful for Your wisdom.

Introduction

Traveling is sexy, especially if you don't do it very often. That's why I was so excited to attend my first real estate investing seminar. I would soon learn everything I needed to know about how to get rich investing in real estate *and* fly across country to do it. OK, Phoenix to Denver isn't exactly across country, but it was still exciting nonetheless. The icing on the cake was that I got to stay at a Holiday Inn—can you say free continental breakfast? Yes, I was a real jetsetter.

It was 2001. I'd worked in the television news industry as a cameraman for the past 15 years. I started out in my hometown of Yuma, Arizona, and then went from Phoenix to Denver, Colorado, and back to Phoenix again in 1995. Each move was strategic. I wanted to make more money and the only way I could was by moving from television market to television market, learning new skills and increasing my value along the way. But by the start of the new decade, I realized that I'd reached the pinnacle of my earning potential as a news cameraman. If I wanted to make more money and have more free time to spend with my wife and future children I'd have to do something radically different.

Desperate for a change, I read Robert Kiyosaki's book, *Rich Dad, Poor Dad*. His message was very clear—the only way a regular guy like me could achieve financial freedom was through real estate investing.

So I did what most newbie real estate investors do. I went online and found a weekend seminar. I spent money on airfare, a hotel room, meals, and ground transportation. I listened to eight different speakers in two days. By the end, I dropped $600 on a lease/option tape set and another $600 on a foreclosure course.

A year went by. I closed two deals and pocketed about $8,000. Not satisfied with my results, I did what most newbie real estate investors do next. I spent more money ($2,700) and flew further away (Atlanta) for a weekend boot camp called "How to Get Lenders Fighting to Give You Money."

Now if the title of this course doesn't make you laugh out loud, then there is something wrong with you. Who would pay $2,700 for something this ridiculous? The dope writing this book, that's who.

Here's what I was told to do that weekend, step by step:

- Find a small community bank.

- Schedule a meeting with the community bank VP.

- Show up to the meeting in a suit and tie.

- Explain to the bank VP that I own a real estate investment business.

- Ask for a line of credit similar to one a furniture store or car dealership gets to purchase inventory.

That's it. The bank VP will then immediately draw up the documents for a $500,000 line of credit to buy an inventory of houses. Believe it or not I tried this—seven times. Nobody was fighting to give me money, but I could swear a few of the VPs I met with were fighting to avoid laughter.

I stumbled around in the dark for about another year. The lease-option-foreclosure thing was going nowhere. And despite my fancy suit and charming smile, the lenders weren't lending, at least not to me.

Out of desperation I called William Kozub, a local real estate attorney here in Phoenix. He had just written an article about investing and I wanted to pick his brain. William gave me the best real advice I ever received, to this day. He told me that if I was serious about learning how to invest in real estate I needed to stop wasting time and money flying all over the country attending these boot camps. He said I needed to learn how to invest from someone doing it in my own backyard.

A week later I enrolled in a short-sale foreclosure course for Realtors. I met a guy in the class who connected me with a real estate investor that was buying houses at the courthouse steps. This investor gave me a shot working for him. He'd give me a list of houses in foreclosure, and I'd knock on their door and ask if they wanted to sell their house prior to the auction. If they said yes, I got paid. My apprenticeship lasted about a year and I learned more (and made more money) than I ever did attending boot camps.

If you want to learn about real estate investing, then find someone in your area that's doing it. Make it worth their while to help you get started. Save the money you were about to spend on the boot camp and buy something worthwhile—like a nice suit and tie. It may come in handy some day.

What This Book Isn't

There is no such thing as a national housing market. Real estate is a local business. Because of this, no two fix-and-flip investors are the same. What works for me in Phoenix, Arizona, likely won't work in Toledo, Ohio, or any other real estate market in the country. This book is not an A–Z plan for fixing and flipping houses. Think of it more like a blueprint. In the following pages, I provide a basic structure for starting and operating a fix-and-flip business. It's up to you to decide how to construct it, how much time it will take, and what materials to use.

I've done my best to include everything I could think of in this book. That said, you'll likely read it and still have unanswered questions. Each distressed home seller and property you purchase to fix and flip will pose its own set of unique challenges. Please accept my apology in advance if I didn't address a specific problem, circumstance, or issue.

I write five to eight times a month on my blog, flippingphoenixhouses.com. Many of the resources I refer to can be found there to download, for free. Best of all, you can contact me there via email with questions, comments, or concerns.

How This Book Was Written

Dr. Philip Rulon could tell a story. He was my American history teacher in college at Northern Arizona University in Flagstaff, Arizona. I actually looked forward to his class. Twice a week, for 75 minutes, Dr. Rulon would colorfully describe important historical events like the Civil War, the Great Depression, and the JFK assassination. He knew so much. It was like he had been there.

Dr. Rulon's lectures never felt like lectures to me. His classes were more like fireside chats—rich with perspective and detail.

He was particularly good with the American presidents. To this day I remember how he narrated the story of Franklin Delano Roosevelt. I sat at the edge of my seat as Dr. Rulon revealed how FDR died—in the arms of another woman at his vacation home in Warm Springs, Georgia. This was juicy stuff and certainly not the kind of information you could find in a history textbook.

One of Dr. Rulon's favorite presidents was Lyndon Baines Johnson, or LBJ. He once told us how after LBJ took office he was asked if he would replace J. Edgar Hoover, the controversial director of the Federal Bureau of Investigation. Dr. Rulon quickly changed his voice into a Texas drawl to imitate LBJ and then answered the question. "No, I'd rather have him on the inside of the tent pissing out then on the outside of the tent pissing in!" The entire class burst into laughter.

When Apress Publishing gave me the tremendous opportunity to write a book about fixing and flipping houses I developed an outline and decided to adopt Dr. Rulon's teaching style into the text—educating through storytelling. I also incorporate this method into the two classes I now teach, "Attracting Investor Clients" (for Realtors) and "Four Flippin' Boxes" (for aspiring fix-and-flip investors).

The very best teachers I ever had used storytelling and their own experiences to educate me. That's what I intend to do throughout this book—use specific, real world examples to illustrate concepts, ideas and processes for successfully (and unsuccessfully) flipping real estate. My hope is you'll gain the insight necessary to start your business or grow your existing business.

This is my story—from company creation in 2002, to domination in 2006, to crisis and chaos in 2008, to comeback in 2010. It's also your guide to navigating the pitfalls of fix-and-flip investing in the post-boom era.

Class is now in session.

Getting Started

CHAPTER 1

Begin with the End in Mind

This is how our business works. Keith sat across from me at his desk and drew four boxes on a piece of white notebook paper. Inside each box he wrote:

ACQUISITION	**REHAB**
SALES	**RAISING CAPITAL**

Keith explained that in order for his fix-and-flip business to operate efficiently—and profitably—he had to have someone dedicated to each box. In the beginning, it was just Keith and his business partner, so they split the four. However, as their company grew they hired staff to help out with all of the boxes—it was the only way they could reach their goal of flipping 20 houses a month.

My church pastor introduced me to Keith in April 2009. I was broke and needed to find a way to survive in the post-boom era. Like a lot of real estate investors from 2004 to 2006, I rode the housing market wave like a drunken surfer. I owned 65 houses (lease-option deals and rental properties I acquired during this time), had a net worth of $8 million, and a bank account with an average daily balance of $175,000.

While I lived in a modest house in a middle-class suburb of Phoenix, I had a voracious appetite for shiny stuff. I bought a $100,000 Mercedes-Benz, a

$65,000 ski boat, and a $10,000 Rolex watch. And because it gets a little toasty here in the summertime I purchased a $400,000 cabin in the mountains near Flagstaff.

Then the music stopped in 2007, and I didn't have a chair. Although my acquisition strategy was conservative (I never paid more than 70% of retail value for a house) there was no way I could know market values here would plummet by more than 60%. By 2009, I had lost my entire real estate investment portfolio. I sold the car, the boat, and the Rolex to help pay the bills. The bank foreclosed on my cabin. My wife went back to work after staying home with my daughters for 5 years, and I went looking for a job.

So needless to say, when Keith and I first met (at a Starbucks, because that's where all real estate meetings take place), I was a financial mess. Little did I know at the time that this would be the most fateful, and profitable, meeting of my life.

Keith did most of the talking. He explained how his commercial and land development businesses suffered—and collapsed—in 2008. However, he and his partner were now doing "something" that was working.

I was surprised by how open and honest he was. Our three-hour meeting flew by without me having a chance to talk about my situation. We made plans to meet again in a few weeks. But just before Keith walked away he asked me about my background. I told him how I had bought and sold over 200 single-family homes from 2002–2006. When the market crashed, my wife and I lost everything.

The following morning Keith called and asked to meet again right away. It turns out that "something" he and his partner were working on was a fix-and-flip business. They were buying homes at foreclosure auctions (known as trustee's sales in Arizona), fixing them up and flipping them for modest profits.

They wanted to expand into another part of town and needed help. Because of my real estate background, Keith brought me on board to help him manage their growing operation. A few months later he would hire me as his Realtor as well.

Of course, I was grateful for the opportunity. The housing market crash of 2008 had wiped me out, emotionally and financially. I needed the cash, and I needed someone to show me how to run a fix-and-flip business in the post-boom era.

It didn't take long for me to figure out how to leverage Keith's success and start raising capital to do my own flip deals. My business partner and friend, Manny Romero, already had cash lined up for us to get started. We flipped 8 houses the second half of 2009, 32 in 2010 and 20 in 2011 (we did fewer last year because we started focusing on higher price points).

Like Keith and his business partner when they first started, Manny and I split the four boxes. My focus is on the acquisition and sales side of the model, while Manny oversees our rehabs and raises new capital so we can do more deals. In 2012, we'll flip around 40 houses. By the end of 2012, our goal is to operate in just one box each, hire staff for the other two boxes, and flip six to eight houses a month.

We have the blueprint to do it. And after you read *Fixing and Flipping Real Estate: Strategies for the Post-Boom Era*, you will too.

Begin with the End in Mind

Make no mistake—fixing and flipping is a business.

Treat this enterprise as anything other than that, and you will fail. I've met a few so-called real estate investors in the past that operated their businesses like a hobby. They started out well enough. But eventually running things fast and loose cost them everything.

Don't run your business like a hobby, because hobbies are expensive. You're not building model airplanes or scrapbooking family photo albums. This is a capital-intensive enterprise that requires attention to detail.

Now, with that little disclaimer out of the way let's get your fix and flip business started. To begin, you'll need to determine what your *income goal* is and then decide what *exit strategy* best suits your personality.

GET YOUR BOOKS IN ORDER

Whether you plan to flip one house a year, or 20, it's important to understand basic accounting principles. I recommend you take a bookkeeping class and use QuickBooks software, or its equivalent, to manage your assets and track expenses. This is especially important if you plan to raise private capital to do more deals (I'll cover this topic later in the book). Sophisticated investors will want to see a profit-and-loss statement and your balance sheet before they invest money.

Income Goal

I net about $10,000 in profit per flip. On higher end deals it's more, but to keep it simple let's just say I net $10,000. If my **income goal** is to earn $120,000 per year I have to flip 12 houses, one per month.

Once I buy a house it takes four to seven days to complete the rehab and another two to three weeks to get it under contract. Most buyers need at least 30 days to close, usually a little more. So, to be on the safe side I estimate it will take 90 days to go from acquisition to rehab to payday.

The average acquisition price for a house that meets my buying criteria is $200,000. If I use a private lender to finance 75% of the purchase price (I'll explain the benefits of leverage in a later chapter) then $50,000 will be required for the down payment. Throw in another $15K–$20K in rehab costs, plus $8K–$10K in holding costs, and the grand total is $80,000 of working capital required.

But $80,000 in cash will only net me $40,000 annually (if it takes 90 days to go from acquisition to rehab to payday then I can only do 4 deals a year). I want to earn $120,000 a year flipping houses.

In order to close one deal a month I'll need $240,000 in cash.

This is where it gets tricky and why it's so important for you to understand how the four boxes work and your role in each one. For example, you may have one house in the remodeling phase, another that's actively for sale and another under contract. While all of this is going on you may have meet with a prospective investor that's interested in giving you some cash to do more deals.

Guess what? You're now operating in ALL four boxes at the same time, and this is perfectly fine. Maybe you prefer to work alone or you lack the financial resources to hire anyone. The point is to understand each role and don't neglect any of them.

How much working capital will you need to reach your income goal? That depends on:

1.   Your target acquisition price.

2.   Your target after-repair-value (ARV) price.

3.   How much rehab is required.

4.   The amount of time it will take to remodel a property.

5.   Whether or not you plan to use leverage (loan) to buy houses or pay cash.

6.   The amount of time it takes to sell a property.

Of course, I have no idea what these variables will be in your market. This part of the equation requires a little homework. I recommend you contact a few real estate professionals (i.e., Realtors, investors, contractors) in your city and find out the ideal retail price point for a house, how much it might cost on average to fix it, and the average days on market.

I also can't tell you what your niche will be. I like newer, cookie-cutter homes that require basic cosmetic repair. You may prefer older, unique homes that require massive renovations. It's up to you to decide the type of property that best suits your personality.

Once you know how much cash you'll need to reach your income goal it's time to get to work. If you already have the working capital required to start, then congratulations!

However, if you're like me (broke) when I started doing this again in 2009 then you'll need to borrow the money, partner with people who have the money, or rob a bank. (I don't recommend the last option—it's really hard to fix and flip houses from behind bars.)

Working Capital Goal

That means you must also set a **working capital goal**, which is the cash you'll need to meet your **income goal**. To visualize these together, I jotted them both down on a piece of paper and posted it on a bulletin board next to my computer to help keep me focused:

- Income goal: $10,000 per month
- Working capital needed to reach my income goal: $240,000

By now you're probably wondering how you're going to find the cash required to meet your income goal. No need to worry—I'll cover that in the raising capital chapter of the book.

Exit Strategies

Real estate investors use a variety of methods to acquire property. However, there are only four exit strategies:

1. Wholesaling
2. Buying and Holding
3. Seller (Owner) Financing
4. Fixing and Flipping

These exit strategies apply to every type of real estate asset class (residential, multifamily, apartments, commercial office space, industrial, and land). While your interest is presumably in fixing and flipping (why else would you be reading this book?), I think it's important to have a basic understanding of all four.

Why? Because chances are you'll be competing with investors that have different exit strategies.

For example, in Phoenix there's intense competition around the $100,000 price point and below. Wholesalers, buy and holders, and first-time and second-time home buyers are all clamoring for homes in this price range. They all can afford to pay more than I can for a property. I have to focus on higher price points ($150K–$300K) in order to get the margins required to fix and flip houses profitably.

I could write a book about each exit strategy. But you're reading this to learn about fixing and flipping so I'll be as brief as possible.

Wholesaling

Buy low, sell low—that's what real estate wholesalers do. I got my start as a wholesaler in 2002. Armed with a list of homeowners in foreclosure, I would knock on 60–80 doors a weekend. If I found a distressed seller willing to sell me their house at a steep discount, I would get it under contract. Before the deal closed, I would find a cash buyer for the house. Then I would do what is known in the business as a "double closing" or "simultaneous closing." The distressed seller, my buyer, and I would all sign on the same day. Therefore, I didn't need any of my own money. This technique allowed me to sell multiple homes at a time for a modest profit (around $3–$5K per deal) without much cash.

Buying and Holding

Buy and hold—pretty simple concept. This is a long-term real estate investment strategy used by investors to generate monthly cash flow and provide an inflation hedge. It's also an excellent way to build wealth.

In a healthy economy real estate prices usually go up around 6% a year. Where they went after the crash is anybody's guess. However, it's reasonable to expect some modest appreciation, especially in those clean, safe neighborhoods with good schools and shopping nearby. Combine rental income, debt reduction, asset appreciation and tax depreciation and you get a safe, above-average return on investment.

I'm a strong proponent of combining a fix-and-flip exit strategy with buying and holding. Prior to the crash, I owned 10 single-family homes that netted about $2,000 a month in positive cash flow. I was able to purchase these properties with the revenue I was generating from my fix-and-flip/lease-option business.

Seller (Owner) Financing

Rent to own, lease to purchase, or buy, sell, and then be the bank by carrying a mortgage note or deed of trust—there are a number of ways an investor can finance the sale of a property to a home buyer. When consumer credit is tight, offering purchase options or financing terms to a home buyer can be very profitable for a real estate investor. I'm a big fan of this strategy in the post-boom era. However, it is illiquid depending on how long a term you offer the buyer.

Fixing and Flipping

Finally, I made it to the good part. Here's what a fix-and-flipper does:

1. Buys low.
2. Remodels.
3. Markets the property.
4. Sells high.

Easy right? Wrong. I believe that fixing and flipping is the most difficult of the four exit strategies. It requires the most cash, technical expertise, and market knowledge.

Fix-and-flippers make their money when they buy, not when they sell. Buying low is the key. The homes they purchase to flip must be discounted steep enough to account for:

1. Repair costs
2. Holding costs (debt service if using leverage, utilities, insurance)
3. Closing costs (title insurance, escrow fees, and loan fees)
4. Commission costs (paid to buyer and seller's agents)

A wholesale buyer, for example, isn't too worried about repair costs. They're not going to fix up the house. A buy-and-holder needn't worry about closing and commission costs because they will lease their property. And an investor that offers seller financing typically pays a lot less for all this stuff because in a tight credit market motivated buyers are in abundance. These buyers are willing to make many of the repairs themselves and pay for the closing costs in exchange for favorable financing terms.

On the other hand, a fix-and-flipper has to account for all four. Therefore, they need to get the very best deal on a property to make a profit.

So how do you acquire the cash, technical skills and market knowledge to successfully fix and flip houses? Keep reading.

Losing Money—Opportunity Costs

I have missed more than 9,000 shots in my career. I have lost almost 300 games. On 26 occasions I have been entrusted to take the game-winning shot, and I missed. I have failed over and over and over again in my life. And that is why I succeed.

—Michael Jordan

Consider:

- Thomas Edison failed more than 1,000 times before he successfully invented the light bulb.

- Abraham Lincoln won a seat in Congress—the second time he ran for office. And Honest Abe was defeated twice more before he finally made it to the Senate.

- Oprah Winfrey was once fired from her job as a TV reporter because her hips were too big. Okay, that's not exactly accurate. Oprah was fired, but she was told it was because she was "unfit." Ironically, she was fit enough to spend 25 years on the air as a talk show host while simultaneously building a $2.4 billion multimedia empire.

History is proof that in order to win in business, politics, sports, or anything else worthwhile, you must be willing to lose. So what about you? Are you willing to lose in order to win?

My investment firm has flipped 70 houses in the last 36 months. We netted about $700,000 in profit. But we lost $170,000 on deals that went bad. How did we lose money? Here are a few reasons:

- I overestimated the value of the home.

- I underestimated the extent of the repairs.

- Values dropped unexpectedly because of the tax credit expiration on April 30, 2010.

- Appraisals came back low.

It's easy for me to look back now and see where I made mistakes. No doubt I'll make more. But I refuse to let failure define me and neither should you.

Most new real estate investors are scared to lose money. That's perfectly natural. You certainly shouldn't invest money you can't afford to lose. But it is unrealistic to think that you'll make money on every house you flip. A deal will go south eventually—sometimes for reasons behind your control. The good news is that being right four out of five times can still be very profitable.

As Theodore Roosevelt once said, "Far better is it to dare mighty things, to win glorious triumphs, even though checkered by failure than to rank with those poor spirits who neither enjoy much nor suffer much, because they live in a gray twilight that knows not victory nor defeat."

Be prepared to lose. It's the only way to win.

Box One: Acquisition

Identifying Your Niche

Some would say I'm boring. Predictable.

I order the same meal, every time, at the Mexican restaurant down the street from my office. When I walk into the neighborhood sushi bar, the waitress doesn't even bother handing me a menu. She knows I'm having the Bento Box B. From microwave popcorn to breakfast cereal to restaurants—it's always the same.

Why?

I know exactly what I want. And when I don't get it I'm usually disappointed.

This is why buying a vehicle can be such a tedious experience. Have you ever walked into a car dealership and told the salesman exactly what you wanted? You explain that the car must be silver with black leather interior, 2-door, convertible, good on gas, and low on mileage. Before you know it, he's showing you everything on the lot but what you just described to him 10 minutes ago.

I can make you a great deal on this minivan, he proclaims. Or how about this jacked-up superduty crew cab pickup truck with gigantic offroad tires and tow winch?

It's easy to say no, because it's not what you want right? Well, if you're like me maybe it's not that easy to say no, especially to a big truck.

Similarly, I also know exactly what I want when it comes to flipping houses. For starters, I'm not into advanced cosmetic repairs or major structural improvements. I prefer quick, easy-to-fix properties that require the basic stuff—carpet, paint, flooring, appliances, landscaping, and minor mechanical repairs. The houses that require major renovations are generally more profitable but require more time and money to sell.

It's up to you to decide. Do you want to do more light, cosmetic rehab deals or fewer big renovation projects? You'll also need to determine the following:

1. Target property

2. Target neighborhood

3. Target price point

4. Target rehab

At some point a wholesaler, Realtor, business partner, owner occupant, or all of the above will attempt to sell you a house that isn't in your wheelhouse. Stick to your guns. Don't be lured into buying a property that doesn't match your buying criteria. Otherwise, you could end up with a lemon.

Target Property

When the latest gadget hits the market, whether it's a laptop, camera, smartphone, or application, I've got to have it. The bottom line is I love new stuff. I love new—or newer—houses too. Thus, my target property is a home built in the last 20 years. Here are my buying criteria (keeping in mind I operate mostly in Arizona):

• Tile roof

• Wood frame construction

• Stucco exterior

• Minimum three bedrooms, two bathrooms, two-car garage

• Home built in 1990, or later

Why tile roofs? They typically last 30–40 years in the dry Arizona desert. When I buy a house with a tile roof, I don't have to factor the replacement cost into my repair estimate. Unfortunately, if you live in the Midwest or on the East coast, there aren't many houses with tile roofs or stucco exteriors.

You've heard that it's hot in Phoenix, right? But it's a dry heat. Most tile roof homes here are built with wood frame construction and stucco exteriors for energy efficiency. Homes with wood frames and stucco exteriors are less expensive to cool in the summertime. Thus, these houses are in higher demand and generally sell for more on a price-per-square foot basis.

Most home buyers in Phoenix, whether they are single with no kids or married with multiple children, want at least three bedrooms, two bathrooms, and a two-car garage. Because a majority of homes in the greater Phoenix housing market don't have basements, people need at least two garage spaces to store all of their worthless junk. Their cars—they park those in the driveway or on the street.

Unless you reside in southern California, Las Vegas, or Florida, your buying criteria will vary greatly from mine. For example, if your base market is Milwaukee, Wisconsin, there haven't been too many houses built in the last 20 years. Nor are there *any* with tile roofs and stucco exteriors. However, you will find lots of ranch-style homes with aluminum siding, asphalt roofs, basements, and block foundations.

Determining a target property is all about comfort—like slipping on a pair of old slippers. Stay true to your guidelines, and you'll avoid unwanted surprises.

Tip: Know what you want in a property—and what your potential buyers want. It simplifies your life and increases your chances of success.

Target Neighborhood

Harold grew up on the south side of Phoenix. Give him an address in zip code 85041 and he can tell you the size of the house and the year it was built. Name a street corner or intersection and he'll recite a historical event that took place there, back to 1950.

Needless to say, Harold knows his neighborhood.

After the market crashed in 2008, he started buying houses in zip codes 85040, 85041, and 85042 for $20,000 to $30,000. These were major rehab projects, but the numbers worked. Harold soon discovered that he could make money flipping houses in one of the roughest neighborhoods in the city.

What's Harold's secret? He knows the neighborhood. And the neighborhood knows Harold.

When an investor buys a house in south Phoenix, guts it, and then installs brand new kitchen cabinets, appliances, HVAC units, carpet, ceiling fans, light fixtures, window blinds, and door hardware, do you know what usually happens next? It all mysteriously disappears—almost overnight.

But that doesn't happen to Harold's houses. Because he personally oversees every remodel job and lets all of the neighbors know it's his house, the cabinets, appliances, HVAC units, carpet, ceiling fans, light fixtures, window blinds, and door hardware all stay intact. I swear, if you drive by one of Harold's properties you'll see a halo hovering just above the roofline. Angels guard his houses.

You see, Harold isn't a greedy investor looking to make a quick buck, he's just Harold—a neighbor and member of the community. So the neighborhood looks after him.

I don't flip houses in Harold's hood. That's by design.

I like to buy in suburbia—in neighborhoods with wide streets, common areas, parks, freeway access, retail shopping and good schools. Homes in these neighborhoods look similar, but they are not identical. Architecture, elevations, and colors share a common theme and are coordinated appropriately. I live in a subdivision that fits this description so I know what buyers like me want in a neighborhood.

Harold and I share the same exit strategy of fixing and flipping our houses. However, our target neighborhoods are completely different. What's important when first starting out is you find an area that you know and feels comfortable.

Target Price Point

Speed is money. How fast do you want to go?

—Jim Boardman (my dad)

The G.I. Joe Jet. Man, did I want that toy. I remember my friend Robby and I drooling over it at the department store the summer of 1984. Together we owned every other figurine and vehicle in the collection—from the Ninja to the Jeep. Unfortunately, we'd never acquire the Jet. At $20, the target price point was too high. By the time we had enough cash to buy it, we'd moved on to a more expensive hobby—BMX racing bikes.

The cash in your bank account will most likely dictate your target price point for acquiring houses to fix and flip. Of course, if you're willing to borrow money to finance some or all of your deal, then you can afford to purchase more expensive properties.

I personally know investors flipping $30,000 houses in Kalamazoo, Michigan, to million-dollar custom homes in Sedona, Arizona, and everything in between. Much like your target neighborhood, your target price point has a lot to do with comfort. You may have the cash to do multimillion-dollar deals. But, the idea of forking out that much money for one property may be more frightening than a colonoscopy.

I buy homes in the $150,000 to $300,000 distressed price range that will sell in the $215,000 to $420,000 after-repair-value (ARV) range. Here's why:

1. There's tremendous competition in Phoenix for homes priced under $100,000. First-time home buyers, second home buyers and buy-and-hold investors are all competing for houses at this price point. Together they drive prices up and reduce potential profit margins for fix-and-flip investors like me.

2. There are fewer retail buyers for homes priced over $420,000. As the list price of a house goes up, the number of qualified buyers goes down. Also, the more money a home buyer has to borrow from a bank to buy my house the more difficult the loan will be to get. I'd rather sell to a larger pool of qualified buyers, so I stick to homes that are easier to afford and are more financeable.

3. Believe it or not, I've found that homes in my target price range require fewer repairs and improvements than those that sell for under $150,000 and over $420,000. How is that?

   • Many homes priced under $150,000 were originally purchased by buyers with little or no money down. They stretched themselves financially and were unable to upgrade their homes or keep up with everyday maintenance. These foreclosed houses are typically located in areas with higher rates of theft and vandalism. It's not uncommon to find a house in this price range missing appliances, HVAC units, and cabinets.

   • Home buyers in the $420,000 range and up are more particular. They expect the best in their homes—from upgraded cabinets, granite countertops in the kitchen and bathrooms, and flooring to gourmet stainless steel appliances. These improvements can be costly and reduce my bottom line.

Some would call this the "lowest hanging fruit" approach to acquiring real estate. I determine my target price point by finding out the answers to these questions:

1. In what price range will I find the greatest amount of motivated sellers?

2. In what price range will I find the greatest amount of distressed properties I can buy at a steep discount?

3. In what price range will I find the least amount of investors competing to buy these distressed properties?

4. In what price range is there an abundance of retail buyers for my fully renovated fix-and-flip property?

5. In what price range can I sell my fix-and-flip property for the highest possible price in the shortest possible time?

Remember, this is not an exact science. I've routinely made $15,000 to $40,000 in profit flipping houses from $52,000 to $420,000. I've also lost $20,000 to $60,000 flipping homes priced from $67,000 to over $540,000.

Regardless of your target price point, keep in mind that while the dollars are different, the principles remain the same. You make your money when you buy, not when you sell.

■ **Note:** You make your money when you buy, not when you sell. In other words, if you buy at the right price, your project is much more likely to be successful.

Target Rehab

The Biggest Loser. American Idol. Extreme Home Makeover. What do these popular reality TV shows all have in common?

Transformation.

Over the course of a few days, weeks, or months, audiences get to witness radical transformations of waistlines, talent, and interior design. It makes for compelling television.

Many fix-and-flippers fall in love with the idea of buying a rundown property and transforming it into a dream home. They become emotionally involved in the rehab, carefully selecting the cabinets, countertops, paint colors, carpet, hardwood flooring, lighting, door hardware, kitchen and bath fixtures, windows, and landscaping features—as if they were going to live in the home.

The process, while oddly romantic and spiritually fulfilling, can be costly and time consuming. At the end of the day, the only thing that really matters is one thing: Can the house be sold for a profit?

This is why identifying your target rehab project is so important. By clearly defining the kind of improvements you're willing and able (or unwilling and unable) to make, you'll avoid getting too emotional about a rehab project. Understanding your strengths and weaknesses (and your team's strengths and weaknesses) is key.

Are you a do-it-yourselfer that's willing to swing a hammer, tear down walls, and crawl in attics? Or would you rather shine a seat with your butt while someone else does all the dirty work? (I prefer the latter of these two, by the way.)

The bottom line is what are you willing to fix or pay someone else to fix? Here's a categorized breakdown to help you decide:

- Cosmetic Repairs
    - Paint
    - Carpet
    - Appliances
    - Lights/Fans
    - Sinks/Faucets
    - Door Hardware
    - Outlets/Switches
- Advanced Cosmetic Repairs
    - Cabinets
    - Countertops
    - Doors
    - Windows
    - Roof
    - Siding/Gutters/Trim
    - Major trim/design
- Mechanical Repairs
    - HVAC
    - Repiping
    - Rewiring

- Advanced Mechanical Repairs
  - Foundation
  - Mold
  - Structural/moving walls/building additions

Rarely do I buy a house that requires advanced cosmetic, mechanical, or advanced mechanical repairs. That's just me. I like to get in and out fast and spend the least amount of money possible on the rehab. However, this may not be possible if you live in a market where the homes are older and subject to harsh seasonal weather patterns. Often times your location will dictate the target rehab.

To summarize, don't get emotional. Know your strengths and weaknesses. Fall in love with the payday, not the transformation.

▒ **Tip**:   Aim to fix and flip houses needing basic cosmetic repairs. Doing anything more takes more time and money, and it increases uncertainty.

3

Analyzing Deals

You've already heard me say it once. However, I'm going to say it again because I had this edict drilled into my head over and over when I first starting investing in real estate.

> YOU MAKE YOUR MONEY WHEN YOU BUY,
> NOT WHEN YOU SELL.

What does this mean? It means getting a great price on a fix-and-flip property will practically guarantee you make money on the sale. Or at least you won't lose money.

Analyzing a deal is part art, part science.

The Art of Analyzing a Deal

A quick thought on the art of analyzing a deal before I get into the science: *You must think like a retail buyer when estimating the ARV (after-repair value) of your property.* This means adjusting the asking price up or down accordingly if the home:

- Faces or backs to a busy street

- Is located on a cul-de-sac lot

- Has north/south exposure vs. east/west exposure (here in Phoenix north/south facing homes are preferable because there's more shade in the front/backyard porch/patio areas during the heat of the day)

- Is a single level, two-story, or multistory

- Sits on a large, private lot

- Sits on a tiny, nonprivate lot

- Has beautiful, well-kept houses next door and across the street

- Has dirty, noisy, or ugly houses next door or across the street

- Has loud barking dogs next door or across the street

These are all locational and environmental factors that could influence a potential buyer to offer more or less money for your property. While these factors may have very little, if any, effect on the appraiser's evaluation of the house, they can be positive or negative selling points for the retail buyer.

Note: You need to take into account many factors besides the condition of the house when making an offer on a house.

By now you may be thinking, how much can a barking dog or busy street really affect the value of a home? Well, a lot. About 10% off the appraised purchase price to be exact (in my area).

The Barking Dog Discount

I bought a house on Cosmos Circle in Scottsdale, Arizona, for $488,000 at a foreclosure auction (known as a trustee's sale). This property was in a highly desirable area with parks, common areas, and a 5-star community center with lighted tennis courts and heated swimming pools. I estimated an ARV of $625,000 and 90 days to go from my acquisition to closing with a new buyer. Five months later I finally sold Cosmos Circle—for $545,000 and a total loss of $59,000.

What went wrong? Did I miss on the evaluation of the house? Did I spend too much on the rehab? Did I underimprove the house for the area? None of the above.

After getting feedback from six different Realtors that showed the home, I learned the real reason it wasn't selling for my asking price—a large barking dog lived next door. One particularly candid agent told me, with a recognizable Brooklyn, New York, accent, "Marty, that f**king dog is costing you a fortune—my client would have made a full-price offer on the house but the damn mutt wouldn't shut up."

So much for man's best friend.

The Busy Street Discount

Then there's the house on Gemini Street in Chandler, Arizona. This bank-owned property backed to a busy road but had a large common area between it and the street. Fortunately, the seller priced it accordingly. Or so I thought. Through careful market analysis, I came up with an ARV of $360,000. To be on the safe side I figured $340,000. I was going to make a killing! After paying $278,000 for the property and spending $12,000 in repairs, $26,000 in closing costs and commissions and $7,000 in holding costs I finally sold it—for $325,000 and a measly profit of $2,000.

Ugh.

Sure, I made a few bucks. But who knew a busy road could make that big a difference to a retail buyer? After all, the house was in a gated subdivision at the end of a cul-de-sac street. I thought that would help make up for the traffic noise. Clearly, I thought wrong.

The Backyard Bonanza

Conversely, buying a property with positive selling points can really increase your bottom line.

I sold a very average home on Newport Street in Chandler for 20% above any other like-property in the neighborhood in one day. I had five offers on the house, four of them above my asking price. The house was your garden-variety three-bedroom, two-bathroom, two-car garage, 2,100-square-foot model. However, it sat on an oversized, private lot with a swimming pool. All of the other homes in the neighborhood were on tiny, postage stamp-sized lots with the houses practically on top of each other.

The Block Party Bonanza

When my wife and I bought the house we are living in now, we paid full asking price. Surprised? I'm supposed to be an expert wheeler-dealer distressed property buyer right?

Not when it came to finding the perfect home for my family. After a long and exhaustive search for a great deal at the foreclosure auction and on the multiple listing service, I decided that our house wasn't an investment, it was a place to live. The home we bought had all of the features we wanted, including 4 bedrooms, 3 full bathrooms, a 3-car garage, and swimming pool.

More importantly, the neighborhood was full of young families like ours that often had block parties. That was a positive selling point—one that didn't show up on the appraisal but motivated us to write a full price offer right after the home went on the market.

■ **Remember:** Sometimes it's not the house itself that motivates a buyer—it can be some of the surprising intangibles that come along with a particular house in a particular location.

Use Online Market Analysis— or a Psychic?

As you can see, there's an art to analyzing a deal. This is why I'm not a huge fan of websites that estimate home values. They're a good starting point for retail home buyers. However, real estate investors need hard numbers and specific property details to accurately analyze the value of a property. It's impossible for a real estate website's algorithms to account for locational and/ or environmental factors.

How could an online site know a huge barking dog lived next door to my flip deal on Cosmos? Or that my wife and I would have paid 10% above the seller's asking price for our house because we love the quarterly block party barbeques? (If you ever tasted my neighbor's mojitos, you'd pay more to live in our neighborhood too.)

No website in the world, with the exception of an online psychic service, could possibly know this information.

And now, finally, I will blind you with some science.

Estimated ARV (After-Repair Value)

In high school and college, math and science were two of my worst subjects. I despised these disciplines so much that I chose a liberal arts degree program at Arizona State University. Ironically enough, I selected Political Science as my major. That's because, contrary to the name, there was virtually no science or math classes required to graduate.

I was progressing quite nicely, halfway through my junior year with a respectable 3.2 grade average, when I learned about a required course called Political Statistics 301.

This class nearly killed me. Call it post-traumatic stress disorder, but I remember just one thing from that dreadful semester. It was a joke the instructor told us at the start of the school year. With a smirk on his face he proclaimed, "Before we begin, remember this: 80% of all statistics are made up."

Of course, everyone laughed. But this professor found nothing funny about my made-up test answers. I barely got out of Political Statistics 301 alive, managing a C- final grade.

How strange for me then to choose the business of fixing and flipping houses, right?

If only my teachers in high school and college would have put dollar signs in front of all those numbers I was forced to crunch. I'm certain my stubborn aversion to math and science could have been overcome much sooner.

Think Like an Appraiser

Estimating the ARV of a single-family home requires some number crunching. You read earlier that determining the ARV requires you to think like a retail buyer. Well, you must also think like a real estate appraiser. Real estate appraisers use three different methods to determine the value of an asset:

1. Income method
2. Replacement cost method
3. Sales comparison method

Income Method

Commercial real estate appraisers typically use the income method. They determine the value of a property by how much income it generates for the owner. After accounting for debt service, property taxes, insurance, general maintenance and cash flow, the commercial appraiser will provide a comprehensive analysis to the customer.

Replacement Cost Method

Insurance companies commonly use the replacement cost method to appraise the value of a property. If your house burns down it really doesn't matter what the surrounding homes in the neighborhood are worth. All the insurance company cares about is how much it will cost to rebuild your home. Before construction begins, you can bet they will hire an appraiser who will use the replacement cost method.

Sales Comparison Method

Residential real estate appraisers use the sales comparison method to determine the estimated ARV for single-family homes, condos, townhouses and mobile homes. They estimate value by analyzing recent sales of comparable homes in the same area.

What does an appraiser consider recent, comparable, and in the same area?

- Recent = 3 months or less
- Comparable = Similar age, style, size, condition
- Area = Within ½ mile of subject property, or less

Your goal is to find similar properties to determine an ARV for the property you want to fix and flip. How do you do that? Follow these steps:

1. Gather specs on the subject property (the house you want to fix and flip)
2. Find at least three comparables (recent, comparable, same area)
3. Collect the specs on these comparables
4. Adjust the value of these comparables
5. Normalize the values and average (you do this by adding to or subtracting from the ARV of your flip property, depending on square footage and other features—how much to add or subtract will depend on your area. I can't tell you how much more value a pool will add to a property in your market, or granite countertops, or a third garage stall. Nor can I tell you how much to subtract if your property only has one bathroom and the others in the neighborhood have two. You'll have to find out by speaking with appraisers and Realtors in your area.)

How do you find comps and collect the specs? Zillow? Realtor.com? County tax records? No. The only true reliable source for this information is your local multiple listing service. And if you're not a member of this service, you can't get access to the data. So you can ask a Realtor in your area to do steps two and three for you, or you can become a Realtor and do it yourself (to which there are some huge advantages).

Three Reasons You Should Be a Realtor and Real Estate Investor

They say you shouldn't eat at least an hour before you go swimming. They also say that two wrongs don't make a right, that you get what you pay for, you can't win them all, nobody ever said life was fair, what you don't know won't hurt you, and there's no such thing as a free lunch.

So who are *they*? I've gone swimming immediately following a big dinner and managed to avoid drowning. And occasionally I get a free lunch paid for by the marketing rep from my title company. I think they are all full of bull fertilizer.

Chances are if you are a real estate investor or are considering getting into real estate investing you've wondered whether or not you should get your real estate license. What do they say about that? When I first started investing in real estate in 2001 I talked to several attorneys and they all advised against it. Why? Two reasons—disclosure and agency.

As a Realtor you are held to a higher standard and therefore open yourself up to potential problems if a real estate deal goes bad. That's why you must disclose that you are a Realtor upon initial contact and later in writing with an agency agreement that states you do not represent the seller of the property. Most importantly, it must be clear that your intent is to make a profit from the transaction.

Contrary to what they said, I decided to get my real estate license in 2007 after operating my real estate investment business for six years. Why did I do this? Three reasons:

1. Access to the Multiple Listing Service (MLS).
2. Increased visibility in the local real estate community.
3. Additional revenue streams.

Access to the Multiple Listing Service (MLS)

From 2003–2006 it was laughable to think that bargains could be had on the MLS. When the bubble burst in 2008, the MLS began overflowing with real estate–owned (REO) and short sale deals. I wanted access to this database. These days, I scour the MLS almost every day searching for and finding good margins. I also use the MLS to comp houses I buy at trustee's sales. I spend about 3–5 hours a day on the MLS and it would be unrealistic to ask a fellow Realtor to do this for me (or use their MLS login info—this is frowned upon by most local Realtor associations.)

Increased Visibility in the Local Real Estate Community

Let's face it, most Realtors know very little about real estate investing. And it's not their fault. The training they get is designed to help them generate business with retail buyers and sellers. That's where I come in. Realtors like to refer deals to me because I'm one of them, and I have real estate investing experience. There are other perks, too. I teach a continuing education class for Realtors at a local real estate school that has helped me grow my database of coaching clients and investor/partners.

Additional Revenue Streams

I do not list the properties I flip. I can't stand working with retail buyers or their agents. However, I do write offers on the REO and short sales I find on the MLS and collect commissions to do it. Occasionally, I have a friend or family member that wants to buy a home and I can refer them to a buyer's agent for a fee. This income isn't too consistent, and it doesn't put food on the table. However, it does make my wife happy—especially if I spend the money on her.

So are there risks in having your real estate license if you are investing? Of course! There are all kinds of risks associated with real estate investing. But, as I've outlined here, the rewards are much greater. As long as you are careful with your paperwork, then those risks are drastically reduced. Just remember if you do end up in court because of a deal gone bad, then you will be held to a higher standard. And I ask what's wrong with that? I didn't become a real estate investor to be held to a lower standard.

Maybe becoming a Realtor isn't for you. Fine. I still recommend you enroll in the licensing classes in your state. Why? Because you know what they say— you learn something new every day.

Terms of Sale

Prior to the real estate market crash in 2008, determining the ARV of a home was much easier. That's because a majority of homes on the retail market were what housing experts call *normal sales*. In other words, these houses were not in foreclosure or owned by a bank.

With the tidal wave of foreclosures that hit nearly every city in the United States, retail markets were overrun by short sale and bank-owned and REO listings. Nowadays, distressed sellers can make up more than 70% of the housing stock in America's hardest hit cities.

This is why, in the post-boom era, there's an extra step required to accurately determining the estimated ARV for the house you intend to flip. There are three submarkets to consider:

1. Normal sales (houses not in foreclosure or bank-owned)

2. Short sales (homeowner owes more than the house is worth, therefore the bank must approve the sale)

3. REO or bank-owned (home has been foreclosed on and is now owned by the lender)

How do you find out if a house was sold by a normal buyer, by the underwater homeowner via short sale, or by the bank? If the property was listed by a Realtor, the MLS description will likely disclose this information. And if you take my advice and become a Realtor you'll know the terms of sale for most properties by looking at the MLS listing information sheet, also known as a Plano.

In Phoenix, for example, normal sales average $100 per square foot, while short sale and REO properties sell for $72–$75 per square foot. Why the discrepancy? There are two reasons:

1. Timing—A seller of a normal home can respond quickly to a purchase offer from an interested buyer, usually within 24–48 hours, and close quickly (15–30 days). Ironically, short sales are anything but short. Even though banks have drastically increased their staffs and improved systems since the crash, it can still take three to six months to get a short sale approved. Buying a bank-owned house is no picnic either. While the process takes less time than a short sale because the lender actually owns the house, there are still lots of hoops for the buyer to jump through. Banks, and their Realtors, aren't that responsive either. It's not uncommon for six to eight weeks to go by before the deal closes.

2. Upgrades and Repairs—Normal home sellers typically make upgrades and improvements to their homes as time goes by. They are also willing to address issues that might come up during the buyer's home inspection. On the other hand, short sale and REO properties are almost always "as is" sales. The buyer can do an inspection, but the seller won't fix anything. The buyer must pay the repair costs.

The "terms of sale" (normal sale, short sale, or bank-owned) can have a huge effect on the estimated ARV of a property. Statistics show home buyers are willing to pay more if they don't have to deal with a bank. How much more?

In Phoenix, about 10%–20%. My hunch is the numbers will be similar in your real estate market.

Here's how the terms of sale directly affects you, the fix-and-flip investor:

- You'll likely be buying distressed short sale and REO properties—properties retail home buyers don't want to hassle with. Luckily, you have the patience and technical skills to close on these deals. Just be aware that the banks move slowly and don't communicate well. They probably won't agree to repair anything to these properties either. Most are "as is" sales. But that's okay; it's why you're getting a good deal.

- Once you have the property all fixed up and back on the market, it will be considered a normal sale. The perceived value for your property is much greater because the seller (you) are a real person that can respond quickly to offers and disclose important information about the house to the prospective buyer.

So, in the post-boom era, in addition to looking for recent, comparable sales in the same area, you'll also want to find normal sales to determine the estimated ARV of your property.

Note: The more you think like an appraiser, the more successful you'll be in your fix-and-flip business.

Case Study: Robin Lane

Now that I've explained the art of analyzing a deal, sales comparison approach, and terms of sale to determine the estimated ARV of a fix-and-flip deal, it's time to put it them all together with a case study.

I purchased W. Robin Lane in Peoria, Arizona, as a short sale for $185,000 and sold it for $245,000 in less than three months. After closing costs and commissions, I net a profit of $23,000. Here are the comparables I used to determine an ARV for the home:

COMP #1	COMP #2	COMP #3	SUBJECT
W. Crystal Lane	W. Melinda Lane	N. 74th Avenue	W. Robin Lane
Sales Price	Sales Price	Sales Price	Sales Price
220,000	265,000	205,000	?
Size	Size	Size	Size
2,296	2,443	2,337	2,337
Bedrooms	Bedrooms	Bedrooms	Bedrooms
4	4	4	4
Bathrooms	Bathrooms	Bathrooms	Bathrooms
2	2	2.5	2.5
Garage	Garage	Garage	Garage
2 car	3 car	2 car	2 car
Year Built	Year Built	Year Built	Year Built
1997	1998	1995	1994
Condition	Condition	Condition	Condition
Excellent	Good	Fair	Excellent
Features	Features	Features	Features
Cul-De-Sac Lot	Private Lot	Private Lot	Private Lot
Pool	No Pool	Pool	Pool
N/S Exposure	N/S Exposure	E/W Exposure	N/S Exposure
Terms of Sale	Terms of Sale	Terms of Sale	Terms of Sale
Short Sale	Normal	REO	Normal

As you can see, all three properties are comparable in size, bedroom/bathroom count, and year built. However, they differ in condition, features, and terms of sale. Note how much less COMP #3 sold for compared to the others. Conversely, COMP #2 sold for $60,000 more than COMP #3 and $45,000 more than COMP #1.

Clearly, COMP #2, while in fair condition and without a swimming pool, was more valuable because it was a normal sale. COMP #1 was, in my opinion, the best comparable to W. Robin Lane because of the similar condition and features. However, COMP #1 was a short sale and short sales were selling in this neighborhood for 10% below normal sales. Thus, I estimated the ARV for W. Robin Lane to be $245,000.

Remember, I fix and flip in Phoenix. It's up to you to figure out how much value to add or subtract for locational and environmental factors and terms of sale in your area.

And one last thing on estimating ARV before I move on: Give additional consideration to the number of homes for sale like yours (also known as active listings) in the neighborhood. Supply and demand ultimately sets the value of a house. Let's look at this in more detail.

Using Active Listings to Determine ARV

An often overlooked but useful value indicator is active listings.

Think about it for a minute. What's the first thing a Realtor will do once their buyer has determined what kind of house they want and where they want to live? The Realtor gets on the MLS and does a search for all active listings that fit the buyer's criteria.

These active listings will be your competition once your fix-and-flip deal is ready to list.

Some of these listings will likely be beat-up short sales and bank-owned homes. A few may be normal sales. Regardless, buyers in the market for a house like yours will be looking at these active listings. How does your property compare?

Before you make a final determination on value for a fix-and-flip deal, always review the active listings in the area. How many are there? How many are like yours? How many that are like yours are traditional sales or remodeled flips? Do they have similar features or upgrades?

Active listings won't tell you what your fix-and-flip deal is worth, but they will give you a good idea of what it isn't worth.

Let's say you come up with an estimated ARV of $125,000 for your property, but there are two to three others just like it on the multiple listing service for that same price. All of them have been on the market 30-45 days. Guess what? Your flip deal isn't worth $125,000 anymore. But a deal may still be doable if you can get the house for the right price.

The Fast Flip Formula

By now I've adequately explained my distaste for math. Formulas, equations, and puzzles make my head hurt.

In the 8th grade, someone gave me a Rubik's cube as a birthday gift. I gave up on arranging the color patterns after 10 minutes. I discovered there was a more efficient solution—disassembling the cube and putting the pieces back together in the proper order.

Needless to say, I'm not going to cook your noodle here explaining how to determine an offer price for a fix-and-flip property. The good news is you don't need to be Albert Einstein. I prefer to keep it simple with my *fast flip formula*:

Estimate ARV – fixed costs – rehab costs – profit = Offer Price

Here's how it works:

100,000	Estimated ARV
– 11,000	Fixed Costs (11% of ARV)
– 15,000	Rehab Costs (what I spend, on average, for a flip deal)
– 10,000	Profit (10% of retail sales price)
64,000	OFFER PRICE

I've already described how to calculate estimated ARV. Now let me explain how to determine fixed costs, rehab costs, and profit.

Fixed Costs

There are three categories of fixed costs:

1. Purchase Costs—the costs associated with buying a property from a distressed seller, which include:

    • Inspection Fee

    • Closing Costs

    • Lender Fees

2. Holding Costs—the costs that come with owning the home during the rehab process, which include:

- Mortgage payments

- Property taxes

- Utilities

- Insurance

- Homeowner's Association Dues

3. Selling Costs—the costs incurred when selling the home to a retail buyer, which include:

    - Realtor commissions

    - Closing costs

    - Home warranty

Rehab Costs

Your rehab costs may, or may not, include the following:

- Demolition costs (debris removal, dumpster, etc.)
- Electrical
- Plumbing
- Cosmetic (paint, carpet, flooring, appliances, yard maintenance, light fixtures, window coverings)
- Advanced cosmetic (cabinets, countertops, plumbing fixtures)
- Mechanical (HVAC, hot water heater, roof)

Offer Price

I'm often asked how much I pay, on average, for a house. Is it 65% of the ARV? 70%? Honestly, I couldn't care less about the percentages. I've paid as little as 54% and as high as 81% for a property and made money.

The biggest variable for any fix-and-flipper is the rehab costs for a house. Obviously, I can afford to pay more for a home that needs $5,000 in repairs than one that requires $30,000 in rehab.

The best way to determine a fair offer price is to create a simple spreadsheet that breaks down all of the fixed and rehab costs for every deal. Don't leave anything out. Once you have all the numbers plugged in, figure out how much profit you desire. Subtract that from your total costs and you've got the offer price.

It may turn out to be 39% of ARV, or 83%.

How much profit is reasonable? Again, that depends on your real estate market. I'm content making 10% of the retail price of the home. That's the baseball equivalent of a single or double. To earn more than 20% of the retail price in profit is a homerun.

Just remember, homerun hitters strike out. A lot.

Acquisition Strategies

In chapter one I identified the four exit strategies for real estate investing:

1. Wholesaling

2. Fixing and Flipping

3. Buying and Holding

4. Seller Financing

However, when it comes to acquiring real estate in the post-boom era for below-market value, there are approximately one bazillion strategies. Okay, that's not really true. But there are a lot, including:

- Buying foreclosures, of which there are three kinds:

    1. Preforeclosures—buying houses directly from delinquent homeowners with equity. It's also possible to buy from upside down, delinquent homeowners via short sale.

    2. Foreclosure auctions—buying houses at the courthouse steps. (Sometimes literally.)

    3. Bank-owned or real estate–owned (REO)—buying homes directly from banks after the foreclosure is complete.

Then there are the other ways:

- **Buying from underwater homeowners not yet in foreclosure.**

- **Buying from absentee homeowners.** These are people who live out of state and are fed up with long-distance property management.

- **Buying from other motivated home sellers.** People that just need to sell fast.

The point is it doesn't matter where you buy or from whom. Just find solid, profitable deals. Think of yourself as a fisherman. Landing the big one requires having many lines in the water.

Foreclosures

Foreclosure. What does it mean exactly? According to Google dictionary, foreclosure is:

> *The process of taking possession of a mortgaged property as a result of the mortgagor's failure to keep up mortgage payments.*

Well stated. Foreclosure is a process, something that happens to a property, not what the property becomes. It really bugs me when I hear someone say, "I want to start buying foreclosures." Really, you want to buy a process? I'd much rather buy a house. There are three phases in the foreclosure process:

1. Preforeclosure. This is the period of time between when the lender officially informs the homeowner that he or she is in foreclosure and the actual auction date for the property. In Arizona, for example, homeowners have 90 days from the day they receive their foreclosure notice (notice of trustee's sale) to either bring their loan current or pay it off. If this doesn't happen, the lender may foreclose on the 91st day.

2. Foreclosure Auction. If the homeowner fails to bring the loan current or pay it off, the lender will foreclose. In many states, these auctions take place at the courthouse steps. If the opening bid of the property is low enough that potential buyers think they can make money in a resale, the home will sell to the highest third-party bidder. These bidders are usually private investors looking to fix and flip or buy and hold. However, more and more people are buying their primary residences at the auction.

3. REO, Bank-Owned, or Lender-Owned. A home in foreclosure will end up in the hands of the bank if no third party bids. This

happens a lot, because lenders usually set the opening by adding the past-due payments, late penalties and interest to the original principal mortgage balance of the loan. Because property values have dropped significantly after the crash, most homeowners owe more than their homes are worth.

You probably noticed that short sales aren't included in the three phases of foreclosure. There are two reasons for that:

1. A homeowner doesn't have to be in foreclosure to do a short sale.

2. If a homeowner is in foreclosure, and is doing a short sale, then it's considered preforeclosure because the bank hasn't foreclosed on the property yet.

Now that you've read this section, you'll avoid ticking me off and sound a lot smarter around your friends. You can make intelligent comments like, "I plan to invest in preforeclosure properties." Or, "Because I have significant cash reserves, I plan to purchase homes at foreclosure auctions."

Since we have that cleared up, let's move on.

Foreclosure: Judicial vs. Nonjudicial States

If your plan is to start acquiring preforeclosures, houses at the foreclosure auction, or bank-owned properties, then you need to understand how the process works in your state.

■ **Legal Disclaimer:** I'm not a real estate attorney. My understanding of the foreclosure process is limited to Arizona, where I operate a fix-and-flip business. I have limited legal real estate knowledge in states not named Arizona. I also have limited knowledge when it comes to blowing glass, building skyscrapers, and doing laundry. However, the latter is by choice. Please consult an attorney or real estate professional in your state for a more detailed explanation of the process.

Judicial States

In **judicial states** like Illinois, New York, and Florida, the lender must take the delinquent borrower to court in order to foreclose on the property. This process can take years to complete. For the real estate investor, buying houses in judicial states can be problematic because the auction sale date is a moving target. It will likely be postponed and changed many times as the case works its way through the legal system. These changes aren't usually published, so the investor must track the sale carefully.

In 2006, I decided to expand my fix-and-flip business to Illinois, specifically McHenry County. As I mentioned earlier, Illinois is a judicial state. I found identifying properties and following them through the process to be extremely difficult. Apparently when judges, attorneys and distressed homeowners get in the same room together, time stands still.

However, if you live in a judicial state there is good news. The less efficient a system is, the more difficult it is to master. The more difficult a system is to master, the fewer people there are willing to master it.

I never mastered the foreclosure process in Illinois. The distance from Phoenix and the housing market crash were too much to overcome. Nevertheless, I found that while tracking sales there was difficult, I didn't have as much competition.

Nonjudicial States

In **nonjudicial states** like Arizona, there are no courts involved. The process is governed by state statute. The lender issues the delinquent homeowner a notice of default (or notice of trustee's sale), and the clock starts ticking. The auction date is published in the notice of default and the whole world is alerted in a very public way. With an auction date set at the start of the process, the homeowner feels a greater sense of urgency, which can benefit the real estate investor.

Of course, with greater efficiency comes greater competition for real estate investors. And not just for preforeclosure deals but at the foreclosure auction and for bank-owned properties as well. Because the process is simplified and easier to follow, investors tend to flock to nonjudicial states like the sparrows of Capistrano.

After the real estate market crash in 2008, nonjudicial states began to recover more quickly because there were few, if any, formal legal proceedings to navigate. Nor were there many robo-signing scandals in nonjudicial states.

Note: To find out if your state or locality is judicial or nonjudicial, get in touch with a real estate attorney in your area.

Acquiring Preforeclosures

I cut my teeth in the fix-and-flip business doing preforeclosures and it all began with a class I took in 2003 called Foreclosure and Short Sales 101. I remember that day well.

The room was full of Realtors, probably because six hours of license renewal hours were being offered. In Arizona, the law requires that all agents take 24 hours of industry-related courses a year to maintain a real estate license. I was not a Realtor at the time so I didn't care about the class credits. However, I was very interested in the subject being taught that day.

The previous year I'd paid over $5,000 to three different real estate investment gurus—for books, tapes, coaching calls and weekend boot camps. Big surprise—none of this material was helping me build a vast real estate empire to dominate the world as I was promised.

There were only a few seats left, so I sat in the back of the classroom next to a large man with a foot-high stack of papers on his desk. The instructor began by explaining that the foreclosure process in Arizona is one of the "rawest forms of capitalism there is." Of course, his proclamation got a big laugh from the audience.

Ironically, that's the only thing I remember the instructor saying that fateful day in 2003. You see, I was too busy watching the big guy sitting next to me. Throughout the class he kept methodically sifting through his big stack of papers, half listening to the instructor while skimming the information on each page.

After about two hours, the instructor announced we'd be taking a short break. Before the big guy could get out his seat I asked him, "Who are you and what's with the stack of papers?" He introduced himself as Mark and explained he worked for a local real estate investor that purchased homes at the courthouse steps (also known as trustee's sales in Arizona). The big stack of papers contained a list of homeowners in foreclosure and map pages with the exact location of each house, including major cross streets.

I asked, "What do you do with these lists and maps?" Mark told me he gives them to his "bird dogs." My next question was, "What the heck is a bird dog?" A bird dog, he explained, is someone who takes the list and map and visits the homeowner in foreclosure. These bird dogs actually knock on the door and ask the homeowner if he wants to sell his house before it goes to sale at auction.

If the homeowner agrees to sell, the bird dog has a purchase contract ready to go on the spot. Once the bird dog has the house under contract he "assigns" it to Mark's investor-employer.

It's a win-win. The investor pays the bird dog an assignment fee, usually around $3,000–$5,000 and in return gets a great deal on a distressed property—a property he won't have to compete with other investors to buy at the auction. Very cool stuff.

I became fascinated with the idea of doing this door knocking myself. I already knew how to search public records for homes in foreclosure and I could easily print out a map page for each property. This would be easy, I thought. All I needed was a purchase contract. I could start buying homes directly from distressed sellers for huge discounts immediately.

When the class ended, I got Mark's phone number and we agreed to stay in contact. The following weekend, with my list, maps, and contract in hand, I started knocking on doors. And believe it or not, it didn't take long to find a homeowner that said, "Yes, I'd like to sell my home."

Excuse me, what?

This distressed seller actually told me, "I want to sell my house." I certainly wasn't expecting that. A few polite "no thank yous," maybe. Lots of doors slammed in my face, absolutely. But never in my wildest dreams did I expect someone to actually say yes. While excited to get a positive response so early on, I couldn't help feeling inadequate. The truth was I had no idea what to do next. I had no idea how to negotiate with the seller or how much the house was worth. Nor did I have enough cash to buy the property.

That's when I remembered my friend Mark with the big stack of papers and his investor-employer. I called Mark up and told him about my dilemma. He asked if I'd like to work for him and his boss as a bird dog. They had the market expertise, title company contacts, cash and buyers to get any deal I brought them done in 24 hours. In return I would get one-third of the profit.

It was an offer I couldn't refuse.

For the next 12 months I worked with this investor and Mark as a bird dog. Every weekend, I'd knock on 60 to 80 doors. By the end of this real estate apprenticeship, I'd close over 20 deals. Meanwhile, I learned practically everything there was to know about doing preforeclosure deals, including how to write a contract, negotiate with the distressed seller, obtain title insurance, build a buyer's list, and keep a house from going to auction minutes before the sale. It was one of the most educational and profitable experiences of my life.

This training gave me the skills and confidence to go out on my own. I didn't need to split my profit three ways anymore. After one year, I had the contacts and the cash to start my own **preforeclosure** business. I would use this acquisition strategy to buy more than 120 houses over the next four years—right up until the market crashed in 2007.

Preforeclosures in the Post-Boom Era

By now you may be thinking, "Sure this worked for you in 2006 prior to the crash when everyone had equity in his or her home, but what about now? Practically every homeowner in the country has an underwater mortgage."

You're smart enough to understand that this works a whole lot better when your offer will cover the seller's mortgage. But not every homeowner is upside down. There are still a few out there that didn't drain every last penny of equity from their home. And life still happens, including job loss, medical problems, divorce, business failure, etc. Regardless of the economy or rising real estate market there will always be people that can't pay their bills. Fix-and-flip investors can't afford to dismiss these distressed equity sellers, no matter how few of them there may be in foreclosure.

Here's how you begin acquiring preforeclosures:

1. Get a list of homeowners in foreclosure. Many title companies provide these lists to real estate investors for free. There are also local and national services that sell foreclosure lists. I'm a Realtor in Arizona and our MLS provides these lists to me as part of my regular MLS service at no extra cost.

2. After you identify the properties on the list that meet your buying criteria, either go to the home and speak with the homeowner directly, or send them a letter. Better yet, do both. The sidebar contains my door-knocking script and an example of a letter I mail out to homeowners in foreclosure. Notice that I never mention I know they are in foreclosure. It's not necessary. The homeowner knows they are in foreclosure and need to sell, so there's no need for me to make an already uncomfortable situation even more uncomfortable.

3. If the homeowner says they'd like to sell after hearing your simple-yet-effective door-knocking script or reading your basic-but-direct letter, then it's time to go through the due diligence process and make an offer on the property. But here's a little tip: Get the homeowner to say how much, best-case scenario, they'd like to get in cash for the house. If it's far above what you're willing to pay, then you know it's not much of a deal. However, they could give you a number far below what you're willing to pay, which is a good thing.

4. Agree on a price and closing date, then get a purchase contract signed by the seller and close the deal as quickly as possible.

DOOR KNOCKING SCRIPT

"Hello, my name is Marty. Is Mr. Homeowner available? I'm a real estate investor and I'm interested in purchasing a few houses in this neighborhood. Would you be interested in selling, or perhaps you know of someone in the area that would? No? Well, if change your mind here's a letter with my contact information."

Example Letter

Hello Homeowner,

My name is Marty and I own a small real estate investment business in Gilbert, Arizona. I'm currently looking for a few houses to buy in your neighborhood. If you've ever thought about selling your home, or know someone who is, please give me a call.

No need to worry about making repairs to your house, cleaning it up, or having a sign in your yard and Realtor lockbox on your door. I'll buy your home in "as is" condition. I'm an all-cash buyer and can close quickly, usually in two weeks or less.

Writing an Offer (Contract) on a Preforeclosure

Contract and disclosure laws vary from state to state. It would be impossible for me to give specific recommendations on how to structure an offer in your state. However, I do have some general tips:

1. Obtain legal advice from a real estate attorney in your area before choosing a real estate purchase contract.

2. Have the attorney review the contract you plan to use and let him or her know how you'll be buying property (directly from a homeowner in distress).

3. Be sure the contract gives you adequate time to inspect the property (usually 3–5 days) and include language that allows you to cancel the purchase if you find anything wrong with the home (this is called a weasel clause because it allows you to weasel out of the deal for any reason).

4. Disclose to the home seller that you are a real estate investor and your intent is to earn a profit from the sale of the home.

5. Keep the contract as simple and as easy to understand as possible.

Important: Don't make an offer without having a local real estate attorney review the language of your contract.

Short Sale Preforeclosures

In the post-boom era, short sale preforeclosures dominate the real estate landscape. I believe it's a perfect storm for fix-and-flip investors like me to gobble up what the retail buying public doesn't want to digest—those homes owned by people with mortgages that are completely underwater.

There's enormous political pressure on the banks to execute short sales instead of foreclosure. It's less expensive and less harmful for everyone involved. The trick is to have multiple offers out at all times, because these deals take so long to close.

■ **Note:**   Bear in mind that short sales take a long time to close.

You can find short sale preforeclosure deals two ways:

1.   By using the methods I outlined above for finding preforeclosure deals with equity (door knocking, direct mail). However, you'll need to work with the home seller and the bank to execute the short sale.

2.   Find an experienced Realtor that can assist you in finding profitable short sales on your local MLS.

I suggest you build a team of Realtors that are constantly scouring the MLS for possible deals. If you are serious, have cash, and can make decisions quickly, there will be no shortage of agents willing to work with you. But, you must make the situation a win-win.

If a Realtor finds a deal for me on the MLS they get to write the offer AND relist the property when the rehab is complete. I also respond within 24 hours to any prospective deals sent my way.

Reverse Comping a Short Sale Deal

In the real estate business, we refer to comparable sales as comps because real estate professionals are way too busy to say comparable sales.

If I'm searching for comparable sales on a house I plan to fix and flip, I call it comping.[1]

---

[1] My spell check says comping is not a word. It suggests I use the word coping, or chomping. But since this is my book, I don't really care what my spell check says. I hereby proclaim that the act of reviewing comparable sales is called comping. Being the author of my own book certainly has its privileges.

Closing a short sale in the post-boom era can be difficult. Across the country, markets are improving and the banks know it. You're wasting your time, the home seller's time, and your Realtor's time, if you don't know how to properly "reverse comp" a house before writing a short sale offer.

Here's an example:

I found 1826 S. Arroyo on the Arizona Regional MLS. The list sales price was $185,000. Before I wrote the offer, I scoured the MLS for comps that would support my offer price of $179,000. I found comparable sales at $165K, $178K, and $192K. These comps were crucial for offer success. The bank ordered a broker price opinion (BPO), and the real estate broker chosen to do the report used these comps to assign a value to the home. If they came back too high, the bank wouldn't accept my $179K offer.

I call this process "reverse comping."

My next step was to find comps that would support an after-repair price of $235–$240K. It took some time, but I found a few traditional sales in this range. But here's the problem: Since I found them, chances are the BPO agent could find them, too, and use them. There wasn't much I could do about that. My only hope was that the broker would take into account that 1826 S. Arroyo was a distressed short sale.

Luckily for me, that's exactly what happened. The BPO came back at 179K. I bought the house, spent $18K on repairs and sold it 70 days later for $250,000. My net profit was $40,000.

That is okiiizzzaay. (All right—I made that word up too.)

Negotiating a Short Sale Deal with the Bank

I'm a distressed-home buyer and fix-and-flip investor. I'm not a short sale negotiator or listing agent, counselor, babysitter, or paper pusher. Thus, I don't get directly involved in short sale negotiations with the bank and neither should you.

When I get a lead through my door-knocking or direct-mail campaign, I refer the home seller to a Realtor with extensive short sale experience. I have a simple agreement with the agent—in exchange for the short sale lead, my offer is the only one submitted to the negotiator. If the bank rejects my offer, the Realtor gets to keep the lead and remarket the property for the bank's approved sales price.

Of course, if my offer is accepted, the Realtor earns a commission and I get a great deal on the property. It's a win-win.

Writing an Offer (Contract) on a Short Sale

I prefer Arizona's standard 9-page real estate contract, written by the Arizona Association of Realtors, when writing an offer on a short sale property. Banks tend to prefer this agreement as well. I don't represent the sellers in my short sale deals, so it's up to their listing agent to explain the contract. If you're working with a local Realtor on a short sale deal, then chances are they'll insist on using the state's standardized purchase contract.

If this is the case, be sure to run it by your attorney first. Typically, these are boilerplate agreements that allow you, the buyer, adequate inspection periods and time to back out of the deal.

Buying at the Foreclosure Auction

So you want to buy a house at the courthouse steps? Remember what my real estate instructor told our class back in 2003? Buying a house at auction is one of the rawest forms of capitalism there is.

■ **Legal Disclaimer:** The process for buying property "at the courthouse steps" varies from state to state. For example, if you're bidding at a foreclosure auction, some states require the purchase be made in cash immediately following the sale, while in other states a deposit is accepted and the remainder of the funds must be paid the following business day. In Phoenix, auctions take place at the courthouse everyday while other cities hold sales monthly.

Again, my experience is limited to Arizona. However, the perils of buying a house at the courthouse steps are similar no matter where you live. This is why I decided to explain, in detail, how the process works here. Some of the terminology and timelines are different, but the risks remain the same.

So here's how it works in Arizona:

First of all, it's not called an auction in Arizona. The legal term is trustee's sale. That's because when a homeowner defaults on their deed of trust (Arizona is a trust deed state, mortgages are not typically used to securitize loans here) a trustee is named to collect the debt. The trustee is usually a law firm or a collection company.

Secondly, these sales don't just take place at the courthouse steps. They occur all over the city in law firms and conference rooms, at 9 a.m., 10 a.m., 11 a.m., 11:30 a.m., 12 p.m., 12:30 p.m., and 2 p.m.. Some trustees do a handful of sales a day while others do hundreds.

These trustees handle all aspects of the sale, from the initial notice to the homeowner (called the Notice of Trustee's Sale), to publishing the notice with the Maricopa County Recorder, to facilitate the sale.

The notice of trustee's sale is sent to the borrower via certified mail and posted in a visible location at the property (usually the front door or garage door). The borrower then has 90 days to either bring the loan current or pay off the debt. If neither occurs, then the property will go to sale.

The trustee, at the direction of the lender it represents, will set the opening bid for the sale. Most of the time, the opening bid is set at what the borrower owes, plus arrears. This is why so many homes end up back in the hands of the bank—no third-party bidder in her right mind would be willing to pay more than what the home is worth.

It's also important to note that few of these sales actually take place on the date written in the original Notice of Trustee's Sale. Many are postponed a week, a month, a year, or longer. This is because the borrower may be working with their lender on a loan modification or short sale. The lender may have other reasons for postponing the scheduled sale (i.e., they already have too many other homes on the market or they think they can recover more money by waiting to foreclose.)

So, if you have your sights set on going to a trustee's sale to bid on a specific property, be prepared to be disappointed because the opening bid most likely will be higher than what you're willing to pay. Or, the sale will be postponed, again and again and again.

At the Auction

There are usually 25–50 bidders at a Maricopa County, Arizona, trustee's sale, most of them professional bidders. Professional bidders can represent numerous clients. Some or all of their clients may be interested in buying the same property. These bidders carry smart phones, tablets and laptops and are in direct contact with their clients during the sale.

Their clients also have different exit strategies. Professional bidders represent primary home buyers, second home buyers, and investors—small, medium and large. These investors each have different exit strategies (fix and flip, buy and hold). Depending on condition, it's not uncommon to see homes sell for 85%–95% of retail value.

The auctioneers don't have gavels, nor do they talk really fast. However, as many as three auctioneers, or more, often will start accepting bids simultaneously so you better know which one of them is handling the sale of the property you want to buy.

Do Your Homework

Before you show up at a trustee's sale, do your homework. For starters, you need to know if the opening bid is set low enough to join the gang down at the courthouse steps. About 60% to 70% of the time, the opening bid is set at what the homeowner owes, plus arrears. As mentioned, this is why so many houses go back to the beneficiary (the bank).

Where do you go to find out the opening bid? If you have a copy of the Notice of Trustee's sale, which can be found on the Maricopa County Recorder's website, there should be a phone number with the sale information. There are also third-party websites that publish this information for free. Many of the trustees have their own websites where you can check for opening bids. The trustees are required to publish the opening bid 24 hours prior to the sale, but they play fast and loose with the rules. Sometimes they'll do a "drop" bid hours or minutes before the sale. If you're not at the sale or you don't have someone at the sale to represent you, you'll have no idea the opening bid was lowered.

Next, you need to know what lien position you're bidding on. If it's anything but the first lien, you'll have to pay off all senior lien holders. Let's say, for example, you bid on a property with an opening bid of $90,000. You bid all the way up to $115,000 and win, only to find out there's a senior lien of $150,000. Guess what? You now have to pay off that senior lien holder to get clear title to the property.

How do you find out what position the foreclosing lien holder is in? You order a title report from a reputable title company or bidding service. The title report will reveal all sorts of stuff—junior lien holders, child support judgments, state and IRS tax liens, Homeowners Association (HOA) judgments, unpaid property taxes, and pending bankruptcy.

Once you're certain the foreclosing lender is in first lien position, it's not a bad idea to drive by the property you want to bid on and make sure it hasn't burned to the ground. If the house is vacant you can probably peek through the windows and over the fence.

In the event the house is occupied you'll have to take your chances. Sure, you could knock on the door, explain to the homeowner that you plan to buy their house at the auction and then ask for a guided tour. WARNING: This tactic usually doesn't work. Expect to have the door slammed on your face or to get punched in the face. If the house is occupied and you win the bid, the homeowner must be evicted, like a tenant that hasn't paid their rent. There are law firms specializing in evicting foreclosed homeowners. This process can be done in about three to four weeks in many states. Of course, you can also bribe—I mean offer cash for keys—the occupant. I've found that $1,000 will get just about anyone to move out in seven to ten days.

█ **Note:** Usually an offer of $1,000 is enough to get a former owner evicted from the house you just bought at auction.

Winning a Bid

The trustee's sale works a lot like a traditional auction. Bids are placed in increments of $100 or more, depending upon how low the opening bid is set and how many bidders are involved.

If you win a bid the auctioneer will require $10,000 in certified funds made out to the trustee. (Again, this is how it plays out in Arizona. Your state or county may do things differently.) The remainder is due the following day at 5 p.m. in the trustee's office. Don't expect a traditional bank to finance the purchase of your property at the trustee's sale. You'll need cash or a hard money loan. There are numerous hard moneylenders in Phoenix that will finance your purchase in 24 hours for 25%–30% down at 16%–18% interest. More on this in the chapters on raising capital.

Taking Ownership of the Property

Congratulations! You won the bid. Except don't expect 30 pages of escrow documents proving you're the new owner. No, all you'll get from the auctioneer is a one-page vesting sheet.

What's a vesting sheet?

Basically, it's a receipt for $10,000 that says you were the winning bidder. The auctioneer will ask how you want the title vested. If you want the title in your name then give them your name. If you want it in an LLC, then give them your LLC's name. It's pretty simple.

In about two or three weeks you'll receive the trustee's deed in the mail. This is the certified document that gives you title to the property. It's up to you to make sure it's recorded with Maricopa County. Don't lose this document. That would be very bad.

And now that you're the new owner of the property you'll be responsible for all of the stuff homeowners have to be responsible for—back property taxes, homeowner's association dues and most importantly, insurance. Whether you're paying cash or getting a hard money loan it's imperative to obtain insurance, especially if there's someone still living in your house.

There are insurance companies that will underwrite a policy on a vacant house—for a steep price, of course.

Buying at Auction: Conclusion

Buying a house at the courthouse steps is not for primary home buyers or the novice real estate investor. You're better off hiring an experienced investor or professional bidding service to help you.

I've been fixing and flipping houses for 10 years and I still use a bidding service. Why? Because I don't have the time to be at the courthouse steps every day. Nor do I have the resources to pull title and drive by 10 to 15 houses a day.

I recommend you visit the courthouse steps or auction location in your market and observe the process. Talk to the bidders. Ask questions. Go back as many times as it takes until you meet someone that can help you understand the process and culture.

Finally, don't fall in love with a specific property otherwise you'll get caught up in the frenzy and overpay. The result will be a broken bank account.

Note well: Never fall in love with a specific piece of real estate. You will end up overpaying for the property.

Buying REO, Bank- or Lender-Owned Properties

The email has been around as long as . . . well, as long as email has been around. It goes like this:

A traveling businessman is having a drink in a bar when a beautiful woman strolls in and sits down. They strike up a conversation and before long the man starts to feel a little tipsy. He eventually passes out and wakes up in a bathtub full of ice. Next to him is a phone, and a note, that says call 911 immediately. After being transported to local hospital the man is informed that one of his kidneys has been removed.

This popular urban legend has been debunked several times. It became so widespread that in 2000 the National Kidney Foundation had to issue a press release to put the general public at ease. They asked for any victims to come forward. None ever did.

A new urban legend was born after the real estate market crash in 2008. Driven by the mainstream media, the general public was led to believe that because of the downturn and global economic crisis, large, medium and small banks all had a liquidity crisis. This liquidity crisis was forcing the banks to sell off their REO properties for pennies on the dollar.

While there was, in fact, a liquidity crisis, it didn't last long. Enacted on October 3, 2008, by President George W. Bush, the Troubled Asset Relief Program (TARP) bought $700 billion of illiquid real estate assets from banks. Here's a list of some of the top players that participated in the program:

1. Bank of America: $45 billion received

2. Citigroup: $45 billion received

3. JP Morgan Chase: $25 billion received

4. Wells Fargo: $25 billion received

5. GMAC (now Ally Bank): $16 billion received

Flush with cash from the bank bailout and other federal loan insurance programs (FHA, Fannie Mae, Freddie Mac), lenders like Bank of America and Wells Fargo were no longer in fire sale mode with their vast foreclosure inventory. Fannie Mae and Freddie Mac got bailed out too. At the time of this writing, these two insurers have received $153 billion.

Another Urban Legend: Bank-Owned or REO Tapes

Unicorns. UFOs. Big Foot. Sasquatch. Leprechauns. The Loch Ness Monster. Everyone has heard of them, but no one has ever seen them. As far as I'm concerned, you can put REO tapes on this list too.

What is a REO tape? It's a package of foreclosed homes that a bank (like Bank of America) or insurer (like Fannie Mae) elects to sell for a discount. The theory is here that by selling them in bulk they solve a big cash shortage problem in a short period of time. The buyers of these tapes (usually hedge funds or private investors with deep pockets) pay from 30 to 67 cents on the dollar per property. Sounds like a win-win right? Absolutely! That is, of course, if you can find one of these tapes. It seems like tracking one of these down is like finding the proverbial pot of gold at the end of the rainbow. Here are a few examples . . .

Where Did the Houses Go?

I ran into a well-connected colleague at a seminar in Scottsdale back in 2010 and he told me that he was about to close a 182-property tape. I asked if he was interested in wholesaling any of these homes to my investment group. He said yes. We spoke two weeks later and the deal blew up. Why? 52 of the homes in the tape had already been sold, and 6 of them had no property tax records.

The Meeting

It took place in a posh conference room in the swanky Gainey Ranch area of Scottsdale just two months ago. My business partner and I were introduced to a very professional gentleman, well spoken and well groomed. He explained that he had connections at both Bank of America and Chase Bank. He could find us one of these tapes consisting of properties that fit our investment strategy. Two months, four emails, and three phone calls later and still no tape.

Tapes or Trash?

In 2009, I met with a California investor anxious to have me help him with due diligence on a 16-property tape he had been offered by a private investment group. Guess what? All but one of the homes had already been sold on the MLS.

In September of 2008, I was asked to do due diligence for a private equity fund on a 78-property tape from Fannie Mae. 38 of the properties were located here in the Phoenix metro area. After conducting a quick search I found that 35 of these homes were listed on the MLS for *less* than the asking price in the tape.

Pie in the Sky

Right around this time I met with one of the leading REO agents in Phoenix. With almost 200 listings, I asked her what kind of discount we could get if I made an offer to purchase all of her Litton Loan listings. She said none and then quickly asked me, "Why would they sell these homes to you for 60–70 cents on the dollar when they can sell them on the MLS for 88 cents on the dollar?" It was a very good question.

So do these REO tapes really exist? Maybe. But don't you think that the bank is going to do everything they possibly can to sell them for top dollar (i.e., at the courthouse steps, on the MLS, at public auctions) first? The homes that get bundled up into these tapes have typically been picked over like the bargain rack at Walmart. They back to major intersections, have power lines in close view, are in war zones, or are in the middle of nowhere.

Now don't get me wrong. I desperately want REO tapes to exist. They would be great for my business. If you can find me one, I'm all ears. It would be like Santa Claus came early.[2]

Have I Burst Your Bubble Yet?

So does all this mean because of the bailouts there are no deals to be had? No, of course not. All I'm saying is that just because the bank owns a house doesn't mean it's highly motivated to sell—at least for a steep discount. In the post-boom era, lenders aren't as desperate to sell as you may think. They're repairing more houses in their inventory, dressing them up with new carpet, appliances, fresh paint, and regular yard maintenance. The end result is a higher offer from a traditional home buyer.

The properties they do let go for pennies on the dollar usually have major cosmetic or structural problems and are located in undesirable areas or back to busy streets.

That said, there are always exceptions. Banks are hard to figure out. Some will steeply discount from time to time. Others do so rarely, if ever. As an investor, there's only one way to find out if a bank is really willing to deal one of their properties: Write an offer.

Writing an Offer on a Bank-Owned Property

No. No. No. No. No. No.

Get used to hearing that word. A lot. If you plan to write offers on bank-owned properties, do not be afraid of rejection. Real estate is a numbers game. In order to get a great deal on a lender-owned property you'll have to write multiple offers. I write as many as 30 to 40 a month.

For a single guy, buying an REO property below market value is a little like asking a girl out on a date. Before I met my wife, I'd have to ask three to five girls out before one would say yes (and for what it's worth, the first one that said yes, I married).

How do you get a bank to say yes to your offer? Let the seller know you are a serious buyer. Now that doesn't mean you make a full-price offer. On the

---

[2] I know he exists because my daughters and I saw him at the mall last December.

contrary, your offer could be considerably lower than the bank's list price. However, the terms of your offer will put the bank's asset manager on notice. Here are some tips for getting a low-ball offer accepted:

1. Offer a large earnest money deposit ($5,000 or more).

2. Let the seller know you can close quickly, in two weeks or less.

3. Shorten the inspection period to 3–5 days (in Arizona the standard real estate contract gives the buyer 10 days to inspect the property).

4. If you really want the property, let the seller know you'll release your earnest money to them after the inspection period is finished. Make the earnest money deposit nonrefundable too. The banks really like that because if you don't close they get to keep your cash.

Using these terms I recently bought a Bank of America property, originally listed at $175,000, for $151,000. Even the bank's Realtor was astonished our offer was accepted.

Just remember, generally speaking, the nicer the house, the less the bank will be willing to negotiate with you. Retail buyers usually purchase houses that are in move-in ready condition. I recommend you limit your search to properties that require light to advanced cosmetic/mechanical rehab. The average home buyer and their Realtor will shy away from homes that require fix up.

The house I picked up from Bank of America for $24,000 below list price needed new carpet, paint, appliances, countertops, landscaping, and light fixtures. Although the total rehab was relatively inexpensive (I spent $16,000 on repairs), few prospective home buyers have that kind of cash for improvements. Thus, my competition was limited to other fix-and-flip investors.

Buying from Underwater Homeowners Not Yet in Foreclosure

The house on Carla Vista Drive had never been remodeled. Nor did the original owner elect to pay for any upgrades when the home was first purchased. Built in 1992, it had no appeal to a retail buyer. From the peach-colored mini aluminum blinds to the blue countertops to the whitewashed kitchen cabinets, this house had it all—all awful, that is.

My wife and I bought it anyway. It was 2004, and my real estate investment business was firing on all cylinders. About $50,000 and six months later, we had transformed this early 1990s eyesore into our dream home.

Soon, my youngest daughter came along. We brought her directly from the hospital to our newly renovated home. She took her first step in this house. Both of my daughters learned to swing on the backyard play set and swim in the pool. On the weekends we'd walk over to the nearby park for picnics.

Then, in 2007, property values plummeted.

By 2008, we were underwater on the mortgage by almost $100,000. Our lender had no interest in a loan modification, and a principal balance reduction was out of the question. So we were left with a difficult decision—throw good money after bad to stay in a home our girls had grown up in, or walk away.

We chose the latter. And now I'm convinced it was an extremely wise business decision.

It didn't feel that way at first. The adjustment was difficult. We had to rent a much smaller home further out of town. Then we had to change schools. There was no backyard pool or park nearby. But, eventually we were able to buy another house again—a home similar to our last, for half the price and payment. Ironically, it was a short sale and the seller was $150,000 underwater. We found out that this family was doing exactly what we did four years ago.

The funny thing is, they weren't in foreclosure yet. Neither were my wife and I when we sold our house in Carla Vista. What most people don't realize is that a homeowner doesn't have to be in foreclosure for the bank to accept a short sale offer.

CoreLogic reports at the date of this book's publishing that nearly 24% of all single-family homes with a mortgage are underwater.[3] That equates to approximately 11.4 million homeowners. Their data indicates that an additional 2.3 million homeowners have less than 5% equity in their homes. That means almost 14 million homeowners have little to no equity in their homes. While CoreLogic's data reveals the number of underwater home mortgages is shrinking (over 25% of all mortgages were upside down in 2011), the problem isn't likely to go away anytime soon.

---

[3] CoreLogic, *Q1 2012 Negative Equity Report,* July 12, 2012, www.corelogic.com/about-us/news/asset_upload_file365_15650.pdf.

▓ **Note:** About a quarter of all mortgages are "underwater" or "upside down"—the house is worth less than the mortgage on it. Though the number is slowly going down, the problem will persist for many years to come.

Strategic Default and Investor Opportunity

What is a strategic default? It's when a homeowner with the ability to make their monthly payment stops paying because they owe more on the mortgage then the house is worth. And it's a strategy more and more underwater borrowers are utilizing.

A patent attorney. A certified public accountant. A physical therapist. A Realtor. A retired utility company worker. A mechanical engineer. A doctor. A nurse practitioner. An elementary school psychologist.

These are just a handful of people I know that have strategically defaulted on an underwater mortgage.

While their backgrounds and occupations are diverse, all are honest, hardworking, and well educated. Each of them, up until they made the decision to strategically default, paid their bills on time and had superior credit scores. They all had significant cash reserves and the ability to make payments on their overinflated mortgage. But it made no sense for them to continue to throw good money after bad. Why? Because it would be decades—or maybe never—before housing values would rise enough to make the investment worthwhile. Of course, their credit scores took a hit. But those can be improved in one to two years. Bad debt can last 20 or more.

I'm not going to debate whether or not this strategy is moral or ethical. All I know is that for the enterprising real estate investor, this trend provides practically endless opportunities. Each one of the people I described above short sold their homes at significant discounts. Imagine how profitable it could be to buy houses directly from these strategic defaulters.

By now you may be wondering, doesn't the homeowner need some type of hardship to get a short sale on their home approved by the bank? Well, yes, and no. You may also be thinking, won't the bank reject the short sale if they know the homeowner can afford the monthly mortgage payment? Well, yes, and no. Many lenders require the borrower have some type of hardship in order approve a short sale. Sometimes the only real hardship is the borrower is underwater on the mortgage. If the borrower stops making the mortgage payment, which they'll likely have to do in order to get a short sale approved, the bank becomes more motivated to accept a short sale offer from an investor like you.

Strategic defaulters aren't difficult to find. Many are already in foreclosure and can be found through a public records search. And those that aren't in foreclosure yet? That's easy. Depending on where you live, most people that bought a house from 2005–2007 are likely underwater on their mortgage. You can search the tax records in your area or pay a lead generation service to find these homeowners. I recommend you send a letter to them, or knock on their door. Use the script and sample letter I provided in the section on preforeclosures.

It's likely they've already considered doing a strategic default. And selling directly to a real estate investor is appealing to an underwater homeowner because they don't have to put a for sale sign in their yard or a Realtor lockbox on their door. They also don't have to scramble to straighten up every time someone wants to see their house.

If you find a homeowner who wants to sell that's not in foreclosure but is upside down, then follow the steps I gave you in the section on buying short sales. The process is the same.

Buying from Absentee Homeowners

Long distance relationship rarely last. Two people can only be apart for so long before the suffering becomes . . . well, insufferable. Eventually, the couple has to break up. So, if it's this tough for geographically challenged lovers to be together it must be nearly impossible for a property owner and their out-of-state property to stand the test of time.

Eventually, the out-of-state property owner falls out love with being an out-of-state property owner. The moment this happens, you want your direct marketing letter to arrive in their mailbox. Here's how it should read:

Dear Out-of-State Property Owner,

My name is Marty Boardman. I've been searching for a home to buy in your neighborhood and came across your name and address after conducting a search of tax records. I noticed you live out of state and thought you might be interested in selling your home. If you don't want to sell please accept my apology in advance. Feel free to use the blank portion of this paper to write a grocery list or to play tic-tac-toe.

However, if you would consider selling please call me at the number below. I'm a cash buyer so I can close quickly. I'll purchase your home as is, no repairs or warranties required.

Where do you find out-of-state property owners? My title company gives me the list for free. You can also pay a lead generation service for this information or search the tax records in your area.

I've learned that not all out-of-state property owners are motivated to sell. Be prepared to field calls from prospects that want full price, or more, for their homes.

Buying from Other Motivated Home Sellers

Life happens. Divorce. Medical problems. Death. Job relocation. Sometimes circumstances require home sellers to liquidate very quickly. Of course, it's difficult for us real estate investors to know where to find these motivated sellers. That's why it's important you let everyone know what you do in a nonthreatening, nonsales way.

Facts tell, stories sell. If you plan to fix and flip full time, use any and all marketing tools available (i.e., business cards and social media like Facebook, Twitter, blog) to market your services. However, DO NOT use obnoxious and overused slogans like WE BUY UGLY HOUSES or I PAY CASH FOR HOUSES. Instead, use these media platforms to document how your fix-and-flip business is helping homeowners out of foreclosure and cleaning up neighborhoods. Use stories, pictures, videos, and testimonials to grow your business.

Be a real estate professional and the other motivated home sellers will want to do business with you.

Common Mistakes

Michelle from Michigan hasn't closed a deal in over two years, though it's not from a lack of effort. The real estate market there is in the tank. It's no wonder she left me two messages in two days for me to call her back. She was excited about finally finding a profitable opportunity.

I explained to Michelle that I've never been to Michigan. I know very little about real estate markets 200 miles from me, much less 2,000. All I could offer her was some objective feedback.

She proceeded to outline the parameters of her deal:

- Custom home located on 3 acres of forest land
- Appraised value at $1.8 million
- Purchase price $1.3 million
- Move-in ready condition
- Owner will carry back the mortgage with 20% down

Michelle gave me a little more information about the area and then asked for my thoughts. I told her I didn't have any thoughts. However, I did have several questions:

- What's your exit strategy?
- What kind of return on investment (ROI) do you want?
- How long will it take you to sell this house?

- If you had to sell the house *fast* what would the sales price be?

It turned out Michelle didn't really have an exit strategy in mind. She may live in the house for a few years and then sell it. Or she could flip it. She hadn't given much thought about an ROI but she was supremely confident the house would sell in about 9 months. Michelle was also very certain the home could be sold quickly for $1.3 million.

Ugh. When presented with any real estate investment opportunity I always try talking myself out of the deal. Michelle was doing the opposite.

■ **Note:** A great way to keep yourself honest and reveal your biases is to try to talk yourself out of the deal you want to make.

Most of her desire to do this deal came from the fact that the owner was willing to carry back the mortgage. Great, I told her. But without a clear exit strategy the terms are irrelevant. What really concerned me was the acquisition price. Michelle said the home would sell fast for $1.3 million and that it's in move-in ready condition. So if she decides to flip the house quickly she'd be paying full market value.

It's important to adopt a "Why I shouldn't do this deal" attitude. This can be tough, especially if you're just getting started or going through a drought like Michelle in Michigan. That's why it's a good idea to get feedback from an experienced real estate investor whenever possible.

The investments I talked myself into cost me the most—in both time and dollars. By the end of our conversation, Michelle understood why this deal wasn't really a deal. She promised to evaluate any future deals with a whole new attitude.

You go, girl.

Mistake #1: Paying Too Much for a Fix and Flip

The most common mistake investors like Michelle from Michigan make is overpaying for a property. I've said before and I'll say it again: *you make your money when you buy, not when you sell.* This is why the first box, ACQUISITION, makes up one third of this book. I want you to clearly understand how to find a good deal and what one looks like when you find it.

Some of the best real estate deals I've ever done are the real estate deals I didn't do. Occasionally, I wish I could go back in time and talk myself out of the bad deals I've done. Remember when I said that writing offers is a little like dating? Get used to hearing "no," right? Well, when someone finally says yes that doesn't mean you run off and get married (although that's what I did when my wife said yes).

However you decide to acquire distressed real estate, whether it be directly from homeowners in foreclosure by direct mail or door knocking, with a Realtor on the local MLS or at the auction, or all of the above, be careful not to get emotional and fall in love with a specific property. Houses are commodities—objects we buy and sell for a profit, nothing more.

▨ **Note:** Again—never fall in love with a house. For fix-and-flippers, a house is nothing more than a commodity that you buy cheaply and sell for a nice profit.

Don't get me wrong, if you plan to start a fix-and-flip business, you will lose money—it comes with the territory. However, it's much easier, at least for me, to deal with a loss if it occurs because of market shifts, project delays, or cost overruns. Losing money because I overestimated the value of the property means I became a little too emotional, too speculative, or both. That's a dangerous game.

Stick to your buying criteria and cost-estimation approach. Use the flip formula I provided, and be disciplined. Don't be afraid of saying no just because the distressed seller says yes.

Mistake # 2: Clouds on Title

Be careful. That distressed property you have under contract to buy may be haunted. No, it's not time to call an exorcist or the Ghostbusters. While the guys in the beige jumpsuits and proton packs are proficient with eradicating those little green slimy ghosts, they are no match for the demons that lurk in that smoking hot foreclosure deal you just tied up.

In the title insurance world, these demons are known as defects, or clouds. I like to think of them as apparitions or skeletons buried beneath the foundation of the house. These clouds vary in size, shape, and form and include:

- Back property taxes
- 2nd mortgage holders

- 3rd mortgage holders
- Mechanic's liens
- Homeowner's Association liens
- State income tax liens
- IRS tax liens
- Child support judgments
- Civil judgments
- Municipal liens
- Bankruptcy
- Lis Pendens (lawsuits pending involving the property or owner of the property)

It helps to think of a house as a magnet. Now regard all the yucky stuff I just listed as metal. When a homeowner gets into financial trouble, his or her home mortgage probably isn't the only bill that's past due. Creditors eventually start recording collections down at the county courthouse. And then they attach themselves to the house—permanently (well, permanently until someone pays them off).

Here's the funniest part about these defects: Most of the time, the distressed home seller doesn't know they exist. Or, more likely, they know a demon exists but don't disclose it to you because of short-term memory loss. Or, even more likely, the distressed home seller just lies about it. Maybe you've heard the expression that buyers are liars? Well, sellers are worse.

Not to worry, though. Your friendly neighborhood *title insurance company* has what it takes to blast the ghosts away. And the title agents won't need to cross the streams of their proton packs to do it either. A simple preliminary title search done prior to closing will uncover any dark, scary objects lurking in the shadows. If there are any liens, judgments, or lawsuits, you'll know. Depending on the numbers, you can pay off the debts as part of the deal. You may even be able to negotiate with the creditor for a reduced settlement. Of course, if an outstanding balance is too high, you can just walk away from the deal.

Most standard real estate contracts include language that will allow you to back out of a deal if there are title issues. Again, be sure to have an attorney review the contract you choose to use to be certain.

Don't ever buy a house without reviewing the preliminary title report. Some investors I know don't buy houses at all without a full-blown title insurance policy that protects against any past clouds or problems that could materialize in the future. I agree it's wise to purchase an owner's coverage policy. However, when buying houses at the auction, it's not always possible. Nor does it work if you're working directly with a homeowner in foreclosure and their sale is 24–72 hours away. A preliminary title report will have to do.

Most title companies will provide reports to investors for little or no cost and usually within one to two business days. Without one you could wind up with a house that would scare a poltergeist away.

Mistake #3: Using Private or Hard Money Financing

I was never late. I always paid my bills on time. The mortgage. The credit card. The car payment. Electric, water, phone and cable—like clockwork every month. Heck, I even paid for magazine subscriptions 3 months prior to expiration.

Then suddenly, in August of 2007, there was too much month and not enough money. My real estate business collapsed faster than you can say mortgage-backed security. I got behind on the mortgages, first on my rental properties and then my personal residence. The credit cards, too. In less than six months my 740 credit score dropped to under 600. Poof. Gone. No more lines of credit or traditional bank financing for me.

Fortunately, things have turned around since then. I'm generating revenue again from my fix-and-flip business, and I'd like to invest the extra cash in a few rental properties. What's a guy like me, with subpar credit but enough cash to put down on a rental property to do? The answer is private money, also known as hard money.

Now I already have a hard-money lender for the fix-and-flip business. Their terms are straightforward: 18% simple interest, $900 loan origination fee. I make monthly interest payments and the loan matures after one year. Expensive? Yes. But I only hold onto the property for 2 to 3 months.

For rental property, I need a lower interest rate to maintain positive cash flow. So I made a few calls and found a local company that will lend at 12%. Good, not great. However, even at 12% interest, with property taxes, homeowner's association dues, and insurance, I have positive cash flow of $300 a month purchasing select properties I find on the MLS.

I started thinking—why don't I use this private moneylender for my fix and flips? The interest rate is certainly better. Then I considered the terms.

The 12% lender charges 3 points and a $900 loan origination fee. In three months, the average time it takes me to flip a house, I'd pay the lender $8,100 in fees and interest on a $120,000 loan. I'd pay $6,300 to my 18% lender for the same deal. As a matter of fact, the 12% loan doesn't become a less expensive option for me until month 7. If it takes me that long to flip a house then I've really done something wrong.

The lesson here is if you're considering a private money loan to fund a deal, no matter your exit strategy, be sure to examine the terms closely. Sometimes more is less.

Box Two: Rehab

CHAPTER 6

First Steps

Sex sells. How else do you think the sitcom *Married with Children*, which ran from 1987–1998, managed to stay on the air for 11 seasons? No, it wasn't the ingenious comedic writing. The show remained popular with the 25-year-old to 36-year-old male demographic for so long because the producers figured out that including scantily clad women in every episode would boost ratings.

Nowadays it's difficult to find anything airing after 7:00 p.m. that doesn't feature half naked women and sexual innuendo—and that's just the commercials. It would be nice to watch the Discovery Channel with my 8-year-old daughter and not have to explain the meaning of erectile dysfunction.

Sexy sells too.

Television has the power to make the most mundane of activities seem attractive. Think of all the reality shows out there today that make ho-hum businesses feel cool: *Pawn Stars*, *Storage Wars*, *Billy the Exterminator*. Since when did killing a cockroach become must-see TV?

To those on the outside of the real estate–investing world, flipping houses is sexy. What's unsexy about buying a house below market, fixing it up, and selling it for outrageous profits? Who wouldn't want to sit around the water cooler at work and brag about making $30,000 on a fix-and-flip? It's no wonder A&E's *Flip This House* is so popular.

Over the past three years, my partner and I have flipped more than 80 houses, many of them purchased at trustee's sales, the rest short sales and bank-owned properties. I can honestly say that there isn't one part of the fix-and-flip process I find to be sexy.

When I win a bid at the auction or get my offer accepted by the bank, I feel worried. Even a little nauseous. Did I pay too much? After the rehab of the house begins, I become impatient. Why isn't it finished yet? Then I get frustrated. Why is the fix-up costing so much? Once the house goes on the market, anxiety kicks in. Why don't I have any offers yet? After an offer is received and I accept it and escrow is opened, I feel uncertain. Could I have got more money for the house if I waited longer? Did I concede too much to the buyer?

Finally, the deal closes and the bank wires me the money, including the profit. That's sexy, right? Not really. Relief is a better way to describe the feeling that overcomes me. Relief I sold the house. Relief I made a few bucks. Relief I have enough cash to do it all over again.

Fixing and flipping houses is not sexy. And rehabbing the house? Well, that's really unsexy.

The Least Sexy Part of Fixing and Flipping

Who could possibly feel sorry for me? After all, I drove a $100,000 Mercedes-Benz. I belonged to the Phoenix Country Club. I wore an expensive Rolex watch and dressed in hundred dollar Tommy Bahama silk shirts. I dined at restaurants like Mastro's Steakhouse without ever bothering to look at the prices on the menu.

That's why it felt a little funny asking my church pastor, Chad Moore, for help after I lost it all in 2008. I told him I wasn't looking for sympathy. No, I wanted to find out if he knew anyone that was going through a similar experience. As fate would have it, he did. Chad put me in touch with a real estate friend named Keith who would eventually teach me the four-box concept of a successful fix-and-flip business.

Keith's system was simple. His company was buying newer homes at trustees' sales that required light rehab and flipping them for a modest profit. He explained that there was high demand for move-in ready homes because of all the distressed REO and short-sale inventory on the market.

You may recall I mentioned in the first chapter that Keith asked me to help him "manage" his fix-and-flip projects, but the job description wasn't nearly that glamorous. I would earn a few hundred dollars a house for making sure the trades got done in four days or less. If I wanted to make more money I could hang the ceiling fans myself—for $10 each. The same for the window blinds, light fixtures and door hardware. They paid me another $125 to clean each property.

I ended up working on 44 houses for Keith in 2009. I logged over 20,000 miles, commuting more than an hour, one way, to the other side of town almost every day of the week. I learned how to hang a ceiling fan in less than

10 minutes and a window blind in fewer than 3. It was physically hard work. Some would even say it was a big step down from my glory days of managing a multimillion dollar investment portfolio. But I never looked at it that way.

I saw an opportunity to learn a new real estate investment strategy from someone with an impressive track record. Yes, I'd have to start at the bottom. That was fine with me because I knew I could use what I learned to resurrect my real estate career.

And I did.

So if you have to unclog a toilet, scrub a floor, pick up trash, commute for hours on end, or fetch someone coffee in order to start—or resurrect your real estate investing career—then do it. Swallow your pride. I've heard it's nonfattening.

■ **Remember:** Swallowing your pride is nonfattening. Do whatever it takes to learn the business and you'll reap many benefits down the road.

Working on Your Business vs. Working in Your Business

Okay, you know:

- Fixing and flipping houses is NOT sexy. (Don't you wish you read this chapter first?)
- Rehabbing a house is the least sexy part of fixing and flipping.

Next, you need to ask yourself a very important question:

Is this fixing and flipping houses thing going to be my business or an odd job?

In other words, are you going act like a business owner and hire employees to perform the work associated with rehabbing the house, or are you going to hire yourself to do everything?

I believe it should be every fix-and-flipper's goal to work on their business, not in their business. My business partner and I don't demolish, paint, lay tile, install appliances, install light fixtures or ceiling fans or blinds, or clean our fix-and-flip properties *anymore*. Our talented team of contractors does this work so we can focus on acquiring additional properties and raising more capital.

However, it's difficult for anyone, regardless of the industry, to work on a business *before* they've worked in the business. Thorough knowledge of the processes and procedures required to get a home fixed up and ready to sell on the retail market is crucial. The best way to learn how to get rehab done is to work for someone who knows how to get rehab done (like I did).

When I worked for Keith, I did everything on his rehab projects that didn't involve wielding a sledgehammer, paintbrush, or plumber's wrench. I quickly learned:

1. What materials cost and where to go to buy them.

2. How long it takes to get jobs done.

3. How to get the jobs done fast.

4. How to get the jobs done inexpensively.

Of course, you can do all the work yourself without any guidance and learn the hard way. Whatever method you choose, the goal should be to replace yourself with less expensive labor once you've learned how to get the rehab done quickly and inexpensively. Then your focus can be on finding and doing more deals.

But what if I like doing all the rehab work myself, you ask? Fine, I say.

There's nothing wrong with getting your hands dirty. I know several local rehabbers who take tremendous pride in their design and carpentry skills. They like working with cordless drills and paint rollers. I've even heard them say that swinging a hammer is a good workout. I say if you can reach your income goals by doing all the work yourself while simultaneously building muscle tone and cardiovascular strength, it's a win-win. Just remember, if you hire yourself as a project manager and laborer you only have yourself to blame if the rehab isn't done on time or to budget.

Starting the Rehab Project

Congratulations! You just closed on your first fix-and-flip project. Now what?

The natural tendency most first-time fix-and-flippers have is to pick up the phone and start calling general contractors, tradesmen, and suppliers for bids on everything from flooring to bathroom exhaust fans.

Easy does it, partner!

While I agree that time is of the essence when flipping houses, there are some important housekeeping items you'll need to address before assembling a team of competent trades (which I'll explain how to do in chapter seven), including:

1. Getting insurance.

2. Securing the property.

3. Turning on utilities.

Getting Insurance

If you obtain a hard-money loan to purchase a distressed property, the lender will require you to obtain an insurance policy and name them as additionally insured. That way, if the house burns down, the lender will receive the money you borrowed directly from the insurance carrier.

For a cash purchase, insurance is not required. When the deed gets recorded, either by you or the title company, you will not get instructions from the escrow agent or a reminder letter from the city to obtain a homeowner's insurance policy. You're on your own.

You must protect your investment. Buy insurance. Do not forget. If your house goes up in flames, so does the cash you spent to buy it.

▓ **Important.** Never fail to buy insurance for your properties. The alternative is to court bankruptcy or worse.

A fix-and-flip property cannot be insured with a standard homeowner's insurance policy, at least not in my neck of the woods. First of all, the house is vacant. It makes insurance companies nervous when no one lives in a house they insure. Weird stuff happens. Appliances, cabinets, air conditioners, and copper plumbing disappear. Sometimes fires start. Roofs leak. Windows break. You get the idea.

There are a few insurance companies that sell vacant home policies. These policies are usually short-term and expensive. However, in most cases they're a fix-and-flip investor's only option. Hopefully you won't have to insure it for too long, three to six months max.

Put in a call to your friendly neighborhood insurance agent. They probably can't underwrite a policy for you but may know someone who can. I purchase insurance coverage from an independent broker that has the ability to shop for the best rates among multiple carriers. That's usually the best way to get a good deal.

Securing the Property

While kicking down a door can be fun and physically challenging, it's not my preferred method for gaining entry into a secured home. The force of the kick usually disintegrates the door and doorframe, adding to the cost of the rehab. The better bet is to hire an experienced locksmith to rekey the house. I trained my project manager to change the door locks, saving me about $100 per house on locksmith costs.

Once all the locks have been changed and the windows are secured, I suggest you put a spare key in a coded contractor's lockbox (you can buy one of these at the local hardware store) and hang it on a hose bib outside the home (never on a door handle because that lets all the thieves know that the house is vacant.) By placing an extra key in the contractor's lockbox you're no longer saddled with the burden of letting every single trade in the house every single time they need access.

Turning on Utilities

It's pretty hard for a plumber to plumb, or an electrician to . . . well, electrify, or the gasman to pass gas (I couldn't resist) without water, electricity, and gas turned on. The initial walkthrough with your general contractor and specialized trades won't go well either if you can't turn on any lights.

Many utility companies require deposits to start service. Consider it the cost of doing business. And you'll get your money back once the house is sold. I recommend setting up an account with each utility provider in your area. With a solid payment history, some of these companies may eventually waive any deposits.

Be sure to arrange for these utilities to be turned on at least two to three days before you schedule the first walkthrough. Some utility companies take up to five business days for new service calls. It would be a shame to have your rehab delayed by a week because the house has no power or water.

▓ **Remember:** Time is money. Don't waste it by dropping the ball here. Get those utilities turned on fast so your trades can get started right away.

Team Building

Edward was the contractor's version of Superman. He was faster than a Skilsaw. His cordless drill was more powerful than a locomotive. The extension ladder he kept in his truck allowed him to climb to the top of a high roof in a single bound.

I had been working for Keith as a project manager about four months when Edward and I first met. During that time, Keith had increased my workload from one house to 20. He had me juggling two to three new rehab jobs a week. I needed help. And not just with the standard stuff like painting, flooring, lighting, landscaping, and cleaning. I needed someone to be *me*—an experienced project manager that could schedule trades chronologically with an eye for what a move-in ready home should look like when finished.

You see, not only was Keith's fix-and-flip business beginning to fire on all cylinders. My business partner Manny and I had acquired our first flip property right around this time as well. So I was now responsible for getting Keith's flips (and my own) completed on time and on budget.

I called Edward from a tiny ad he placed in a tiny newspaper I found outside a grocery store exit. He was a handyman, plumber, electrician, painter, and regular jack-of-all-trades—exactly what I needed at the time.

Now I wasn't about to use Edward for any of Keith's rehab projects. I couldn't risk my new project management position, a flexible job that had already paid me more than I had earned in the past 12 months, by hiring a contractor I didn't know anything about. Imagine if Edward turned out to be a complete loser. You know, one of those multiple personality types that shows up on time the first day and then disappears for weeks on end, inevitably pushing the job past deadline and over budget. This would have cost me my job. So instead, I hired Edward to work on my own first fix-and-flip deal. If he was going to go postal it was going to be on our job, not Keith's.

The property was located in Maricopa, Arizona. This bedroom community, located 30 miles south of Phoenix, was hit hard when the housing market collapsed. Values plummeted by more than 70%.

We picked up the house at the auction, sight unseen. Well, sort of. My dad lives in Maricopa so I had him drive by the property the morning of sale. After determining the home was vacant, he peeked through some of the windows and reported that everything looked to be sound on the inside. Later that afternoon I arrived with a locksmith. And much to my chagrin everything was not sound on the inside.

The home had been gutted—the original kitchen cabinets, bathroom vanities, sinks, toilets, and light fixtures had all been removed (stolen). But mysteriously, all of this stuff was replaced with cheap, used material. There were kitchen cabinets in place, but they were old, beat up, and didn't fit properly. The appliances were ugly, mismatched and broken. In the master bathroom there were pedestal sinks where the vanities used to be (leaving the new homeowner with no place to store towels and toiletries). Even the tub had been removed, replaced with an unfinished fiberglass shell. All in all, this home would require a complete makeover. Ugh.

In need of a cold drink, I retreated to the local grocery store where I picked up 64 ounces of orange Gatorade and a free circular with Edward's tiny little advertisement. I called him, and we met at the home the following day.

He showed up on time, which if you know anything about contractors is an epic accomplishment. Edward and I walked through the house and I pointed out each job I needed done, including:

- Finishing the master bathroom tub

- Putting trim around the plantation shutters in the family room and kitchen

- Hanging light fixtures throughout the house and installing door hardware

I would project manage the flip myself and subcontract out the rest of the work like the kitchen cabinets, countertops, carpet, landscaping, and cleaning. Edward quoted me a very reasonable price for the work and finished it all in three days.

Over the next six months I would give Edward more and more work. The work consisted of my rehab projects first but eventually included Keith's fix-and-flip deals too. It took about ten houses for Edward to learn exactly what we wanted a property to look like when completed.

I still remember the day I turned all of the project management duties over to Edward. We had breakfast at the Cracker Barrel in Buckeye, Arizona. Buckeye, like Maricopa, was decimated by the housing market crash and was fertile ground for fix-and-flippers like me. Between Keith's company and mine we were turning six to eight houses a month there, mostly in a subdivision called Sundance located off the I-10 freeway about 30 miles west of Phoenix.

As Edward and I finished devouring our pancakes and eggs that morning I finally popped the question. "Edward, will you be our full-time project manager and general contractor?" Of course, he said yes.

The relationship continued to grow and blossom the next two years. He repaired garbage disposals, rewired wall outlets, replaced broken roof tiles, refinished kitchen cabinets, installed new kitchen cabinets, and hung drywall. I bought a house once with a missing kitchen cabinet drawer. Rather than search the city for a replacement Edward made a new one in his garage and matched the stain perfectly. I could trust him to select and purchase thousands of dollars of material at Home Depot or Lowe's. And when he called to tell me a house was ready to list for sale, I knew it was ready to list for sale. The home would smell like apple pie (from the cinnamon air spice air fresheners he put in the wall outlets), and the carpet always had those cool V shapes from the vacuum cleaner.

Yes, Edward could do it all. But alas, our bond was not strong enough to stand the test of time. You may have noticed throughout this chapter that I've been referring to Edward in the past tense. After two years of investor-contractor togetherness he vanished, virtually overnight. Poof. Just like that, he was gone.

Manny and I were about to start the biggest rehab job we had ever undertaken, and Edward never showed up at the property. A few days later I would find out from our landscaper that Edward had left me for another customer in another state. I never got a phone call, text, or email from him. Superman broke my heart.

Hiring Contractors and Tradespeople

Contractors, tradespeople, handymen (and handywomen)—they are a different breed. I've met and done business with hundreds of them and the only thing many of them seem to really care about is getting the next job—ideally a bigger, better, higher-paying job. A lot of contractors become so focused on landing the next project that the one they are currently working on (yours) gets delayed, goes over budget, or both.

▓ **Note:**   Look for contractors who don't have their eye on the next job as they complete yours.

Understand that once you start fixing and flipping houses, you'll never stop hiring and firing project managers, carpenters, electricians, painters, landscapers, roofers, plumbers, cabinet installers, pool cleaners, and designers. Your relationship with these trades will likely grow, blossom, wither, and die, much like bad marriage. It's not inevitable, but it's highly probable. Here's the eight-step evolution of an investor/contractor relationship:

1. The Blind Date

2. The Courtship

3. The Engagement

4. The Rehearsal Dinner

5. The Wedding

6. The Honeymoon

7. The Marriage

8. The Divorce

The Blind Date

It helps to think of the start of an investor/contractor relationship as a blind date. Maybe a friend referred a painter to you. Or perhaps you found a carpenter on Craigslist. My favorite way to find a reliable, inexpensive tradesperson is to get a referral from a contractor I'm already working with. Good contractors like to work with other good contractors.

As I mentioned earlier, the first woman I asked out that said yes, I married. I wasn't kidding. My wife and I started dating when I was 21. I was engaged at 25, married at 26. Needless to say, I've never been on a blind date. However, I have several friends that have been on blind dates.

Here's how one of them describes blind dating:

> The two interested parties show up at the agreed-upon location in their best clothes. Both are well groomed. Neither will reveal much about their character, religion, political views, or favorite sport teams out of fear they will offend the other person. Or worse, completely gross them out. If there is any chemistry, a second date is planned immediately following their first date. Contact information is promptly exchanged and schedules are checked for future availability. If there is no chemistry both agree to

"stay in touch" and then permanently erase all traces of the meeting from their memory.

It's a good thing I never had to go out on a blind date. I love to talk about politics and my favorite NFL football team, the Arizona Cardinals. And while this sanitized approach may help find love, it won't help you establish a successful business relationship with a reliable, inexpensive contractor.

When blind dating a new contractor I follow the age-old real estate adage, "Disclose, disclose, disclose." In a very courteous and polite tone, I let the contractor know that I'm a real estate investor and can't afford to pay retail prices for labor and material. I also explain that time is of the essence. I have a budget and deadline to meet. However, I promise to pay immediately after job completion and more future repeat business if my project is finished on time.

Tip: Be as honest as you can up front about the nature of the job, what you expect, payment terms, and so on.

This disclosure starts the relationship off in a professional manner and helps the contractor understand I'm not a typical retail client that will bog them down with micromanagement and frequent change orders.

The Courtship

If the contractor understands my needs and is comfortable working for a wholesale customer, then negotiating for services can begin. I really don't like making tradespeople bid against each other to win a job, but it's a necessary evil when first starting out. Just remember, price isn't everything. For example, if a painter agrees to paint the exterior of my house for 85 cents per square foot but can't start for three weeks, then I'm better off hiring a painter that charges 95 cents per square foot and can start immediately.

I like to tell a new contractor that I'll likely get two to three bids for the project and I'm looking for a combination of low price and efficiency. This usually results in two to three competitive bids. Now I'm left to decide which contractor is best mentally equipped to get the job done.

This isn't easy and I've been fooled before. I look for people with a positive, can-do attitude and a sense of humor. I like contractors that are decisive, independent thinkers but aren't afraid to ask me questions about the project. They can handle the little stuff without calling me 20 times a day yet are humble enough to contact me about the bigger issues. Sometimes you won't learn this stuff until you've done a few jobs together.

The Engagement

With the courtship over, it's time to get engaged. Terms, pricing, and schedules are agreed upon in this stage of the relationship. The good news is you can spare the diamond ring, rose petals down the hallway, and chocolate on the pillow. The contractor you choose to spend the rest of the project with would prefer you just stay out of the way. And pay on time.

Depending on the size of your fix-and-flip project, you may want to provide the contractor with an independent contractor agreement and a scope of work document. (See appendix for samples of these documents.) A scope of work is a detailed description of the work you want the trade to complete. I've found that a scope of work isn't necessary for basic cosmetic rehabs that include paint, flooring, appliances, light fixtures, and landscaping. However, if your rehab includes major structural, electrical, plumbing, roofing, siding, windows, foundation, or grading improvements, I highly recommend you use a scope of work. It helps you to create a project schedule and coordinate the trades accordingly.

■ **Tip:** Having a scope of work document you share with your contractors can save you a lot of trouble later on.

You'll also need to provide each contractor with a W-9 tax form.[1] Why? The IRS wants to know how much you're paying these contractors for their services. At the end of the year, you'll provide these W-9s to your accountant, along with the amount you paid each trade. Be sure to get the W-9 signed and returned before you pay the tradesperson for the job. Otherwise, you may never get it back. If a contractor refuses to sign the W-9, then you need to find another contractor. Chances are they are skirting the IRS.

The Rehearsal Dinner

No, you don't need to buy contractors anything to eat. Although I've heard rewarding workers with a cooler full of beer at the end of a long day can really help improve morale. The rehearsal dinner in rehabbing is called the *walk through*. Before I begin any new project I like to get as many of the contractors

---

[1] Department of the Treasury, "Request for Taxpayer Identification Number and Certification," December 2011, www.irs.gov/pub/irs-pdf/fw9.pdf.

that are available to meet me at the property to review the scope of work, the schedule, and, most importantly, the deadline. I like to walk through the house, point out specific areas of concerns and ask for suggestions.

This exercise keeps everyone on the same page and opens up communication between all of the trades. If your deadline is tight (it should be) then multiple contractors will be working inside and outside the home at the same time. They will need to work well together and coordinate their schedules accordingly.

For example, if you've scheduled a painter and flooring contractor to be at the house on the same day then they need to work around each other. They can start at opposite ends of the house, or on different floors to avoid bumping into each other.

The Wedding

Okay, so now you've ironed out all of the details. I now pronounce you investor and contractor. No kissing, please.

The Honeymoon

This is my favorite stage of the investor/contractor relationship. Everyone is happy. I'm excited because I found a motivated tradesperson that can complete the job quickly and inexpensively. The contractor is happy because he found a savvy, decisive real estate investor and the potential for future business.

The rehab moves along like clockwork. All of the trades show up on time and get along splendidly. The budget and deadline is met. When I gather all of the trades back at the property for the final walk through, I find everything listed on the scope of work has been completed exactly to specification.

This means champagne and caviar for everyone. But again, no kissing.

The Marriage

In this phase of the relationship the investor and contractor settle into a routine. They know each other's strengths and weaknesses. They complete each other. Once I've made it to the marriage stage with my trades, I know I can count on them to show up and finish the job on time. Trust has been established.

I feel comfortable sending my project manager to Home Depot to purchase materials like ceiling fans, light fixtures, door hardware, window blinds, and light bulbs without blowing the budget. I know my painter won't miss making obvious drywall repairs. I can count on my landscaper to choose just the right amount of flowering shrubs for frontyard curb appeal.

▧ **Note:** You know you're in the midst of good marriage when you trust contractors to make decisions and buy on your behalf.

Of course, there's an occasional breakdown in communication. But for the most part everyone does what he or she is supposed to do. So much so that the initial walk through may not be necessary.

The Divorce

Sooner or later, you'll become disgruntled with a trade. Or, they'll become disgruntled with you. Here are some key indicators that a divorce with your contractor is eminent:

1. Contractor displays a lack of attention to detail.
2. Contractor is unable to complete a job on time as promised.
3. Contractor is unable to complete a job on budget.
4. Contractor calls you an idiot.
5. Contractor doesn't call you at all.

Why does this happen? Human nature, I guess. You'll likely discover that once contractors have won your business, they can become complacent. They miss the small stuff. They get busy with other customers and neglect your project.

Remember my long lost project manager Edward? The last few jobs he did for me were substandard. I remember scheduling a final walk through with him for a property located over an hour from my office. When I showed up at the house, the painters were still there painting. I asked Edward if he understood the definition of the word final. Nothing ticks me off more than when I schedule a final walkthrough with my project manager and the job is not complete.

Of course, contractors may elect to divorce you. Here's why they would choose to do that:

1. You don't pay on time.
2. You don't pay enough.
3. The contractor found a bigger and better deal.

Neglecting to pay your trades promptly is bad. I like to pay mine within seven days of job completion. Likewise, if you squeeze contractors too much on price, then they'll ditch you and your project when a more lucrative opportunity comes along. (I'll have tips on how to negotiate pricing with trades in chapter nine.) And even if you pay on time, and pay fairly, nothing will stop a contractor seeking out a bigger and better deal.

Where Did Edward Go?

Eventually I would learn that Edward got a bigger and better deal. I found out from my landscaper that he moved to Canada to build log cabins for a wealthy land developer. Thus, I can't blame Edward for leaving me. No doubt his new employer offered a steady paycheck, benefits, perhaps even a brand new cordless drill and extension ladder.

Still, a phone call, text message, or even a Dear John letter would have been nice.

Licensed vs. Unlicensed Trades

As the property owner, it will be up to you to decide whether or not to use licensed or unlicensed trades for your rehab project. There are pros and cons to both.

Licensed tradespeople are required to carry insurance, which protects you, the homeowner. If a licensed plumber burns your house down with a torch, then his insurance covers the damages. If a licensed painter falls off his ladder and gets hurt, then his insurance will cover the medical bills.

Those are the pros for using a licensed trade. The biggest con is the cost. Licensed trades usually charge more for their services because they have the costs associated with being licensed, as well as the insurance expense.

Unlicensed trades, on the other hand, have no insurance costs, so they can charge much less for the same quality of work. However, if an unlicensed roofer breaks his back falling off a ladder at your house then you could be on the hook for the hospital bill.

If your flip deal requires building permits of any kind, then the city will likely require that your trades be licensed and bonded with the state. Some municipalities even require trades be licensed with the city the house is in as well as the state.

It's important to note that just because a contractor is licensed doesn't mean he or she is good, and just because a contractor is unlicensed doesn't mean he or she is bad. Over the years I've employed both in my fix-and-flip business and have settled on this criteria when deciding whether or not a trade should be licensed:

Trades That Must Have a License:

- Plumbers
- Electricians
- Roofers
- HVAC (air conditioning and heating contractors)
- Painters (it depends)

Trades Where a License Is Optional:

- General handyman work
- Flooring (carpet, tile, hardwood)
- Pool maintenance and repair
- Landscaping maintenance and repair
- Painting (it depends)

As you likely figured out, for the big, mechanical stuff I like to use licensed trades. Many investors I know also insist on using licensed painters. Why? Painters use tall ladders and are prone to fall off of them from time to time. Currently, the painter I use is unlicensed. However, he's fast, inexpensive, reliable, and good so that trumps the risk exposure. I'll take my chances on any ladder mishaps.

The licensed vs. unlicensed trade question all boils down to comfort level. Are you willing to pay more for peace of mind or would you rather roll the dice on using an unlicensed, uninsured trade that saves you thousands on the project?

If you're like me, you'll probably settle on using a combination of both.

CHAPTER 8

What to Fix

It's tough being me.

Every day I wake up and wonder—should I wear shorts and flip-flops or jeans and dress shoes? Then I have to decide if I'm going to work at my office or at a remote location (i.e., Bergies Coffee in downtown Gilbert, Arizona, because that's where all the movers and shakers in the area go to work and drink). By lunch time, it's do I eat the leftover pot roast or splurge on the taco plate at Baja Fresh? And when I get home, do I relax with a beer or glass of red wine?

So many decisions.

Decisions, Decisions

I have a similar dilemma whenever I purchase a house to fix and flip. Do I replace the existing 12" tile with 20" tile? Should I get rid of the laminate counter tops and install granite? Are black appliances okay or do I upgrade to stainless steel?

Most real estate investors I know struggle with knowing exactly how much, or how little, to spend on their rehab deals. That's because if the house isn't fixed up enough, it won't sell. And if too many improvements are made, the profit margins disappear.

So what's the secret sauce? How do you find a happy medium? The answer is simple. Well, sort of.

Start by finding the most recent pending or closed comparable for your fix-and-flip deal. Make sure it's not a dumpy short sale or bank-owned property. Do your best to find a regular sale. Next, review the local MLS and pictures for this comparable. Drive by the house, too. Go inside if possible (if it's still on the market as a pending listing). Make mental notes of what was, and wasn't, done, to the property. Better yet, take real notes.

If the intent is to sell your flip for the same price, or slightly higher than the last comparable, then guess what? You need to make identical improvements. If the plan is to sell your flip for significantly higher than the last comp (a risky bet because your deal may not appraise for a higher list price) then additional upgrades will be necessary.

Tip: Find a house comparable to your fix-and-flip deal that sells for the same price you want to eventually sell your house for. Then upgrade your fix-and-flip to that standard.

Last fall, I bought a fix-and-flip in an upper-middle-class neighborhood of Phoenix from a bank for $340,000. A Realtor brought the deal to me. He had an identical listing on the next street over pending for $450,000. So before I bought the REO, we took a tour of this property. We decided that if I could remodel the $340,000 bank-owned stinker for $30K–$40K and make it look like his $450,000 model-like home, then money could be made.

After purchasing the property in late October, my crew had the house sparking in less than two weeks. I put granite countertops in the kitchen and all the bathrooms, tiled the showers and bathtubs, installed all new light fixtures and plantation shutters on the windows, and put an epoxy coating on the garage floor. Half of the backyard was concrete so we jackhammered it all out and put in grass with decorative curbing.

I listed it at the beginning of November. And the home sat. And sat. And sat. And sat. No offers.

After a series of price reductions I finally got the house under contract in February of this year for $410,000. Now there were a number of factors not related to the remodel of the home that affected the sales price, the most important being the time of year it was listed for sale. Unfortunately, many home buyers in this price point stop shopping around the holidays.

Once the new year passed, interest grew in the property and I received several offers, including the buyer who ended up buying the house. However, there was no way, despite renewed interest, I could remarket the property at $450,000 again. I'd already played my hand. Since last spring, when I finally flipped this property, listings in the area have resumed selling in the $440,000–$460,000 range.

What can I say? Timing in real estate is everything. At least I can sleep well knowing I fixed all the right stuff.

What to Fix: The Four Categories of Repairs

As you just learned, repairing all the right stuff still may not always result in the profitable sale of a fix-and-flip deal. But imagine what would have happened if I didn't upgrade this home adequately? How much money would I have lost then?

Recall that in chapter two, I broke down the four categories of repairs a fix-and-flip property may need before it can be remarketed and sold for the highest possible price in the shortest possible time:

- Cosmetic Repairs
  - Paint
  - Carpet
  - Appliances
  - Lights/Fans
  - Sinks/Faucets
  - Door Hardware
  - Outlets/Switches
- Advanced Cosmetic Repairs
  - Cabinets
  - Countertops
  - Doors
  - Windows
  - Roof
  - Siding/Gutters/Trim
  - Major trim/design

- Mechanical Repairs
  - HVAC
  - Repiping
  - Rewiring
- Advanced Mechanical Repairs
  - Foundation
  - Mold
  - Structural/moving walls/building additions

Keep in mind that these repair categories are not mutually exclusive. I've rehabbed houses that required mostly minor cosmetic repairs but also kitchen cabinets. I've also worked on houses that fell into all four categories.

■ **Tip:** Think of repairs in the four categories listed above. It'll simplify your life—and your deal.

Cosmetic Repairs

Whether you buy a house at the auction or purchase a short sale from the MLS, it's likely you'll need to do at least some very basic cosmetic repairs to your property. I've spent from $1,800 to $12,000 replacing carpet, tile, appliances, light fixtures, door hardware, ceiling fans, and window blinds. Typically you can buy this stuff at Home Depot or Lowe's. Consider yourself lucky if you find a great deal on a fix-and-flip deal that requires less than $5,000 in cosmetic repairs.

Advanced Cosmetic Repairs

I specifically look for houses that require advanced cosmetic repairs. Why? First of all, the average home buyer doesn't have the skills, cash or imagination to buy a property that needs kitchen cabinets, countertops, windows, a new roof, and siding or exterior paint.

A few years ago, a Realtor called and asked me if I had any houses I was in the process of fixing up. I explained to her that I was always in the process of fixing up houses. After this agent gave me her buyer's criteria I let her know about a home I just started rehabbing that might have the size and features they were looking for. The Realtor took her client to see the home the next day, and guess what? They didn't buy the house. One could argue it's because the house wasn't quite right for the prospective homebuyers. I think the real reason they didn't write an offer is because they couldn't picture the house all fixed with brand new granite counter tops, carpet and fresh paint. Instead, the Realtor and her clients saw a beat up property with nasty carpet, ugly countertops, and cheap fixtures.

Another reason I prefer houses that require advanced cosmetic repairs over those that need mechanical and advanced mechanical repairs is cost. It's much easier to budget for things like carpet, paint, kitchen cabinets, roofs, doors, and windows than it is for stuff like plumbing, electrical, and structural improvements.

Lastly, few cities or municipalities require a homeowner obtain building permits for advanced cosmetic repairs. This will dramatically reduce the amount of time and money required to complete the job.

Mechanical and Advanced Mechanical Repairs

You'll find that some of the best deals to be had are on those houses that require intensive mechanical and advanced mechanical repairs. Even the most seasoned real estate investors I know shy away from properties that need major plumbing, electrical, or structural repairs. Why? Fear of the unknown.

Let's just say when you start tearing off sheetrock and ripping off roofing material there are usually surprises hidden underneath—and not the good kind of surprises, either. I once had a $75,000 rehab budget balloon to over $100,000 because of major structural and electrical issues that no one on my team could have known were there until the flooring was removed.

What's more, when you purchase a property that requires mechanical and advanced mechanical repairs, you'll likely need to get building permits. This can add lots of time and money to your project costs too.

All that said, I rarely turn down a great deal, regardless of the rehab budget. Remember, there's no problem that price can't fix.

Note: Houses needing advanced mechanical repairs will sometimes surprise you and not in a good way. Unexpected expenses come with the territory when you embark on a fix and flip business. Roll with the punches and you'll come out okay in the end.

Choosing the Right Project to Begin

I don't recommend starting your real estate investment career by purchasing a home to flip that requires advanced mechanical repairs. Stick to the simpler stuff. Sure, you can probably make more money on a per-deal basis by flipping houses that require major overhauls, but the tradeoff is they take longer and cost more to fix up.

What if you can't find any houses in your area that only require advanced cosmetic repairs? Then buy a less expensive house. At least that way you won't have as much cash wrapped up in the deal.

My partner and I average about $12,000 in profit per deal on houses that require advanced cosmetic repairs. We know investors that average $25,000 in profit per deal flipping houses that require mechanical and advanced mechanical repairs. In the end, we all make about the same amount of money on our flips.

How is that possible?

My partner and I spend about $14,000 per flip on repairs and sell our houses in less than 90 days. The guys we know doing the major rehab deals are spending $30,000 to $50,000 and are holding them for up to 5 months or more. So we can often do two deals in the time it takes the major rehabbers to do one.

■ **Remember:** Turning houses over faster enables you to make the same profit as those who make bigger profits on a house but who turn them more slowly.

It all boils down to your market, your skill set, and your bank account. How good are you with either fixing stuff yourself or finding trades that can? And how much cash can you afford to spend fixing these houses up? How long can you keep it tied up? Your answers to these questions will dictate what type of repairs you can afford to make.

The "Pow" Outfit

My brother, Curtis, needed a suit. And since he was a 25-year-old news cameraman residing in Phoenix, Arizona, his closet was devoid of any fashionable formal wear. Our family was about to embark on a seven day/night cruise to the Mexican Riviera. One of these evenings on the ship would be spent sipping champagne and dancing in the ballroom. If Curtis showed up in a t-shirt, shorts and flip-flops to the captain's party, no doubt access would be denied.

So he did what any guy would do—he went to the Men's Wearhouse because he wanted to like the way he looked.

The salesman advised my brother that he needed a "pow" outfit. "What's a pow outfit?" Curtis asked. "A pow outfit," the salesman explained, "is an outfit that says *pow*! People see you in this suit and are instantly impressed with your sense of style."

My brother left the store that day with a sharp looking sports coat, mock turtle neck shirt, and stylish slacks. And when we all saw him for the first time that night on the ship in his new duds? Well, pow! The kid looked like a cover model for *GQ* magazine.

The "Pow" House

Like my brother's cruise ship apparel, when completed, your fix-and-flip property should go "pow!" To earn maximum profit, the prospective home buyers' senses must be overwhelmed when they walk through the door.

So what does a "pow" house look like?

Take a tour of any new model home. That's the standard you're aiming for. The floors are clean, the carpet is freshly vacuumed, the walls, trim and baseboards are painted, the windows sparkle, and the appliances shine. Even the wall outlets and doorstops look brand new. The front and backyard landscaping are manicured. And don't forget the air fresheners—preferably apple cinnamon.

Do you know why there is a new car scent option at the car wash? Because people love to be reminded of how their car smelled when it was new. The bottom line is we all love new stuff and the fragrance of new stuff. That's why a house that looks and smells new will usually sell more quickly.

If you pay attention to the small stuff and don't cut any corners, the homebuyer will like the way the house looks—I guarantee it.

The point is if you're going to fix and flip a house, then do it right—whether it's a simple paint and carpet job or a major overhaul. With all of the resources home buyers have at their disposal these days it's important to not cut corners. They'll notice.

Pow!

CHAPTER 9

Cost Control

The overloaded orange hand truck was filled high with ceiling fans, light fixtures, door hardware and faux wood miniblinds. I made my way slowly from the Home Depot pro desk to the parking lot, careful not spill any of the precious cargo.

Yes, I could have made two trips to the car with my stuff. But that's not how I roll. I'm a guy, and guys get it done in one trip, not two.

I loaded the items into my chariot, a 2004 Chevy Tahoe with the back seats folded down, like a master puzzle solver. Each box was arranged so that not a spare inch of space went unused. Just as I was about to put the last piece in place (the light bulbs because they are delicate), a man approached.

I wonder when a total stranger appears out of nowhere in an empty parking lot at 6:30 a.m. Is this random person going to shoot me? Ask for money? Jumper cables? Directions to Lowe's?

Instead he asked if I was going to install the ceiling fans, light fixtures, door hardware and faux wood miniblinds myself. The thought crossed my mind, I said. The man told me he was an electrician and could do all of the work in three to four hours. Naturally, I asked what he would charge. Without hesitation this parking lot solicitor said, "$400."

Wow. $400. For 4 hours of work. I know doctors who don't get paid that well. When I broke down the math out loud the man quickly revised his quote. "I'll do it for $150," he said.

I learned a valuable lesson in the Home Depot parking lot that day. While material costs (i.e., cabinets, countertops, windows, doors, ceiling fans, blinds, etc.) are pretty much fixed, labor costs are very negotiable. By asking the contractor for a price and estimated job completion time, I quickly determined how much he was getting paid per hour. And $100 per hour was way too much to hang a few ceiling fans and window blinds.

These days I ask all new contractors, "How much and how long?" If there are material costs included in their bid, I ask for those to be separated from the labor costs. Then I know exactly how much I'm being charged per hour. For the typical handyman type of work, $25–$35 an hour is reasonable.

Of course, when dealing with licensed trades like roofers, electricians, and plumbers, all bets are off. Most have set hourly rates. But, I've found even those can be negotiated. I've had success lowering my labor costs for HVAC and major appliance repair just by asking "how much and how long?"

When the laborer has to really think about what they are charging on a per hour basis, their perspective may change a little—which puts a little extra change in my pocket.

■ **Tip:**   The question "How much and how long?" directed to contractors, can save you a lot of money over time.

Negotiating with Trades

I'll admit that I'm a lousy negotiator. I hate haggling over prices. My dad, on the other hand, will ask for a deal wherever he shops. He'll go into places with fixed pricing like Best Buy, Home Depot, or the Apple Store and negotiate with the salespeople. The funny thing is, he'll usually get some kind of bargain.

For example, my dad recently bought a new iMac computer. Apple won't negotiate price. However, they do offer discounts on their products to students and teachers. He mentioned to the sales associate that my mom retired from a community college about five years ago. After some consideration the salesman determined that they qualified for a $100 discount on the computer purchase. Not bad.

I've learned that with contractors, tradespeople, and handymen, there's a fine line between getting a fair price for quality work and getting completely screwed. If you beat up a trade too much on price they'll never want to work for you again. If you pay too much, you'll lose money. So with that, here are five tips for negotiating with trades:

1.   Meet the contractor at the home and explain the scope of work.

2.   In a nice way, let the contractor know you'll be getting at least two to three estimates.

3.   If you're planning to do more rehabs in the future, be sure to let the contractor know that as well. More work will come their way if they can provide fair pricing and speedy work.

4. Once the contractor has seen the job, always ask how much and how long. Get them thinking about an hourly rate.

5. Choose the contractor that provides you the best combination of customer service, price, and scheduling. Remember, time is money. It's counterproductive to find an excellent trade that can't start your job for two to three weeks.

You'll quickly discover it's easy to weed out the slackers using this five step process. Let's say you call three or four painters to bid out an exterior paint job. At least one of them won't show up at all and one or two will be late. Chances are you'll also get one ridiculously high bid. Hopefully, the obvious choice will then present itself.

▧ **Tip:** Always get at least three or four estimates for any job you need done on one of your houses. You'll be amazed at how they vary.

Fixed Pricing

There are a number of standard fixes and upgrades you'll be making on almost every fix-and-flip deal you purchase. These include:

- Paint
- Flooring (carpet, tile, laminate, hardwood)
- Light fixtures
- Door hardware
- Window blinds
- Countertops
- Appliances

In the beginning, you'll probably have to bid out this work. However, as you develop a track record and build rapport with trades, you can dictate what you'll pay. I now have fixed pricing for each of these items.

- Paint: $0.75 per square foot (interior and exterior), and this includes materials
- Flooring: $3.25 per square foot for tile installed, $10.95 per square yard for carpet)
- Light fixtures: $10 per fixture

- Door Hardware: $35 per house, regardless of how many doors

- Window blinds: $10 per blind

- Countertops: $35 per square foot for granite installed

- Appliances: $1,300 for the range, microwave, and dishwasher installed

Agreeing up front with contractors on pricing for standard fixes will make estimating repairs costs *before* you buy a property much easier.

Fixed Material and Supply List

Another great way to save time and money is to have a fixed material and supply list. This will require you to visit stores and write down the product SKU numbers. However, it's worth the effort. Not only will you have a picture in your mind of what each item looks like, but you'll also identify the best finishes for your property (i.e., satin nickel vs. oil-rubbed bronze light fixtures). When my project manager goes to Home Depot or Lowe's for supplies he has a spreadsheet for:

- Ceiling fans

- Door hardware

- Light fixtures, including coach lights, kitchen and dining room chandeliers, bathroom vanity lights, and flush-mounted hallway fixtures

- Window blinds

- Plumbing fixtures

- Appliances

This cost control measure, like fixed pricing for trades, will assist you in determining a budget prior to starting the rehab.

Keeping Contractors and Trades Happy

In chapter seven, I explained how working with contractors and tradespeople is a lot like a bad marriage. I've met countless carpenters, plumbers, electricians, painters and landscapers that were extraordinarily talented. However, they had limited customer service and scheduling experience. Finding an affordable contractor with good people skills is a rare combination. If you find one, then be sure to do your part to maintain the relationship.

For example, whenever my project manager or trades do a great job, I let them know. I remember their names and give them Christmas cards with cash bonuses at the end of each year. Occasionally, I'll even drop off a cooler of beer at the job site (Friday nights only). Of course, the very *best* way to let a contractor know that you love them is to pay on time.

Tip: Pay your contractors on time. It will endear you to them and they will do better work for you.

Underimproving

In an effort to control costs, many investors underimprove their properties. Rather than replace dirty, worn-out carpet, they have it cleaned. They keep dated fixtures and appliances. Some investors will slap a coat of interior paint on a house and put a for sale sign up in the yard. While this strategy may be profitable from time to time, over the long run it's not sustainable. The market can tell when all you're really doing is putting lipstick on a pig.

For what it's worth, this is not fixing and flipping. If you don't have the money to fix a house up the right way, then you're gambling that a retail buyer will purchase your property in spite of its condition. Think about it like this: If all your property really needs is a carpet cleaning and fresh coat of interior paint, then why didn't a retail buyer snatch it up? Even the most unimaginative home buyer can operate a steam cleaner and paint roller.

A fix-and-flipper adds value to a distressed property. If you don't add enough value then the homebuyer will be unwilling to pay your asking price. And even if you find someone willing to pay your asking price, it's unlikely an appraiser will see the value added. Your deal could blow up because the appraiser determined that the difference between what you paid for the house and the retail purchase price is too great and the improvements you made were too small.

Remember: Your job is to add enough value to the property to attract a retail buyer—and satisfy an appraiser that the asking price is fair.

Of course, there are exceptions to this theory. I've gotten lucky with making minimal repairs to properties ($2,000 or less) while still earning a healthy profit. However, these deals are difficult to find and are balanced out by the houses that require massive "surprise" renovations.

So how do you avoid underimproving a house? Compare, compare, compare.

Remember that REO property I told you about in chapter eight? Before I purchased the house, I went to a similar property on the next street over that was already under contract. I took note of the kitchen and bathroom upgrades, window coverings, and fixtures. I had to be certain that my property had similar finishes. If you buy a distressed property and choose to keep the existing carpet and kitchen cabinets, install linoleum flooring, white appliances, laminate countertops, and brass light fixtures, then don't expect it to sell for the same price, or more, than the same house down the street with new carpet, kitchen cabinets, hardwood floors, stainless steel appliances, granite countertops and oil-rubbed bronze light fixtures. Trust me, you'll be disappointed.

Overimproving

You've probably seen this car on the road before—a late model import with a colorful, fancy paint job and an abundance of accessories. Its spinning chrome wheels, exhaust pipes, and bumpers glisten in the afternoon sun. The aftermarket spoiler, positioned strategically on the trunk, rises high above the roofline, making the vehicle look less like a car and more like an oversized shopping cart.

They say beauty is in the eye of the beholder. No doubt that Disco Dan, the owner of this pimped-out driving machine, believes his automobile is the envy of the neighborhood. After all, he spent more money accessorizing the car than he did to buy it. Unfortunately, Disco Dan will be in for a rude awakening after he gets married, has children, and is forced to sell his rad ride for a minivan with a built-in DVD player and luggage rack.

The general buying public will not be impressed with his car's bountiful bling. There is no premium placed on chrome wheels or rear spoilers. As a matter of fact, Disco Dan's over-the-top upgrades actually devalue his asset.

How so?

A normal buyer will have to calculate the expense of returning the car to normal in their offer price. These expenses will include a new paint job, wheels that don't spin, and the removal of the obnoxious rear spoiler. In the end, Disco Dan will be fortunate to get 10 cents on the dollar in return for the so-called "improvements" he made to his rainbow on wheels.

It's possible to overimprove a home too. I call them "Disco Houses." Their owners go over the top with accessories—everything from wall-to-wall travertine tile bathrooms and tongue-and-groove ceilings to cultured stone interior walls and exterior elevations. While these finishes may look stunning in a million-dollar mansion, they are way too over the top for a $100,000 suburban tract home.

Not long ago, a Realtor I work with sent me an REO listing in Peoria, Arizona. It had been on the market about 30 days and was priced competitively. For the life of me I couldn't figure out why this property hadn't been snatched up by a retail buyer. Then I saw the pictures and the song "Stayin' Alive" started playing in my head. This was a white-leisure-suit-black-collar-gold-chain-wearing-John-Travolta disco house.

It had oversized crown molding and baseboards throughout, lavish light fixtures, and antique bathroom vanities. Every surface in the kitchen was covered with cultured stone, travertine, or granite. Based on the price, size, and neighborhood, the previous owner had gone completely overboard with the upgrades—so much so that a regular homebuyer couldn't afford to unimprove all of the improvements.

While certainly more rare than underimproving a home, I have seen fix-and-flip investors (and normal homeowners) go the other direction and overimprove a property. It's not necessary to install granite countertops, oil-rubbed bronze fixtures, and travertine showers in an $80,000 property. Few homebuyers will see the value in these kinds of upgrades and an appraiser probably won't either. Worst of all, overimproving a house will eat into your budget and erode profit margins.

Here are two tips for making sure you don't overimprove a property:

1. View other comparable properties in the neighborhood (preferably other flips or normal sales), and take note of their improvements and finishes. Use similar ones for your deal.

2. View new home models and take note of their designs, paint schemes, and finishes. Homebuilders pay professional designers big bucks to decorate their houses, so copy what they do for your properties.

This approach has been profitable and cost effective for me. I encourage you to employ a similar strategy. Perhaps together we can put the Disco House to death. Forever.

Common Mistakes

The road to successfully fixing and flipping a profitable deal is paved with unforeseen problems, unexpected booby traps, unknown pitfalls, and hidden landmines. While there are common mistakes that occur in all four boxes, the ones that happen within **Box 2: Rehabbing** can be the most frustrating and difficult to avoid.

Why?

Because the circumstances that lead to many of these mistakes are beyond your control. How well you and those on your team adjust, smoothly and efficiently, to these setbacks is the key to avoiding losing money on a deal.

Taking Too Much Time

Punctuality is the thief of time.

—Oscar Wilde

So how long should it take to fix up a house? Well, that depends on the type of property you purchase. Here are some general guidelines:

- Cosmetic Rehab: 3–7 days

- Advanced cosmetic rehab: 7–15 days

- Mechanicals: 2–3 weeks

- Advanced: 2 weeks–2 months (or more)

There are two reasons why taking too much time to complete a rehab can be catastrophic:

1. Holding costs.

2. Opportunity costs.

If you're paying interest to a debt partner, private mortgage lender, or bank for some or all of the purchase of the property, then *holding costs*, including the mortgage, property taxes, utilities, and insurance, will destroy your bottom line very quickly.

Let's say you finance $100,000 for a fix-and-flip deal at a 15% simple interest rate. Here's what the numbers look like if it took you eight months to sell the property:

$10,000	8 months of interest payments
+ $1,000	Property taxes
+ $900	Utilities
+ $600	Insurance
$12,500	**Total**

Hopefully you calculated this $12,500 expense into your formula before acquiring the property. Every now and then I'm approached by a wholesaler or Realtor with a "great deal." They estimate repairs and profit but leave out the holding costs. As you can see from the example above, holding costs can erase your projected profit very quickly.

But how could it be possible take 8 months to rehab and sell a house you ask? It's easily done like this:

1. You're lazy, unmotivated, indecisive, aloof, uninterested, unorganized, constantly tardy, or all of the above.

2. Your contractors are lazy, unmotivated, indecisive, aloof, uninterested, unorganized, constantly tardy, or all of the above.

The simple solution is to not be some, or all, of the above, or to not let your contractors be some, or all, of the above. There are four things you can do to help prevent taking too much time to get the job done.

1. Provide your trades with a project schedule and scope of work.

2. Show up at the house occasionally, but don't get in the way.

3. Be decisive.

4. Immediately fire any contractor that doesn't show up on time or complete the job on time as promised.

Keep in mind, even if you provide contractors with schedules and show up at the house every day, there will still be problems that neither you nor anyone on your team can predict. For example, I once lost 10 days on a large rehab project near Milwaukee, Wisconsin, because the city's building permit department thought that my carpenter's license had expired. It was a simple misunderstanding that took a brief phone call to clear up but it added almost two weeks to the job completion time. On this same property, I ran into several structural issues that weren't uncovered until the drywall was removed. Additional engineering work had to be done that added even more delays.

There are also *opportunity costs* associated with taking too long to get a property fixed up and sold. If all your cash is tied up for six to eight months rehabbing a property, how many great deals will you have to pass up during this time? One? Three? Ten? As painful as it is to break even or lose money on a flip because it took too long to sell, the real kick in the gut comes when you start thinking about all the other profitable deals you couldn't buy.

▒ **Tip:**   Fire any contractor who doesn't show up on time or doesn't complete the job on time.

Paying Too Much

They say money talks. All mine ever says is goodbye.

—Red Skelton

"You have a deviated septum." That's what the doctor said to me. Have you ever broken your nose, he asked. No. He then explained it's possible my nose developed this way over time. How does that happen? Well, if you combine an already somewhat crooked nose with a rash of sinus infections, you may end up with a deviated septum.

Based on my doctor's diagnosis, I scheduled an appointment with an ear, nose, and throat specialist. My ENT doctor concurred. I did in fact have a deviated septum that required surgery to repair. A CAT scan would be needed first to determine the extent of the damage.

Now, I'm self-insured. So whenever I hear the words CAT scan and surgery together I get nervous. In 2005, I had ACL surgery on my knee. That little procedure cost me $5,000—my entire family insurance deductible for the year.

When I showed up at the hospital's outpatient clinic, the lady working the front desk cheerfully informed me that the copay for the CAT scan was $658. My insurance company would pick up the other 80% of the bill. Isn't that nice? If my math is correct, that's about $3,290 for a procedure that takes 4 minutes.

I asked Ms. Cheerful what the CAT scan would cost if I paid cash. She didn't know. I asked her to find out. After about 10 minutes of waiting she called me back to her desk. It would be $912 cash. Of course, she reminded me, if I paid cash none of it would go towards my insurance deductible.

Then I really started thinking. If I wanted to buy a new TV or digital camera would I do it at the first place I stopped? No. Shouldn't I shop around to get the best price on a routine medical procedure? Needless to say, I called another clinic down the street and they quoted me a cash price of $225 for the CAT scan. That's where I had it done. No wonder health insurance reform is such a hot topic right now.

One of the biggest problems with being new to fix-and-flip investing or starting a fix-and-flip operation in a new market is not knowing how much it should cost for materials and labor. That's why it's so important to shop around. Many investors are in such a rush to get their rehab started that they only interview one or two contractors for each job. Or worse, they accept the first bid the contractor offers without any attempt to negotiate a lower price.

Don't be that investor. Shop around and do what I suggest in chapter nine by always asking your trades, "How much and how long?" Then hold them to both answers and ditch those who fail to live up to their end of the bargain.

■ **Remember:** The magic words for finding the right contractor: *How much and how long?* Then expect them to meet their promises.

Substandard Finished Project

Good judgment comes from experience, and a lot of that comes from bad judgment.

—Will Rogers

The retail home buyer, or the retail home buyer's Realtor, will probably let you know if your house hasn't been remodeled properly. Unfortunately, by the time this happens the horse is already out of the barn.

I once flipped a high-end property in north Scottsdale. After 30 days on the market, I decided to call a few of the Realtors that showed the property to find out why they never submitted an offer. Several of them told me that the exterior of the home needed to be repainted. When my project manager and I did our initial walk through, neither of us thought it was necessary. Clearly, we thought wrong.

Buyers in the higher price points have a more discerning eye and can easily detect when the home seller is cutting corners to save money. My bad decision to skip the exterior paint job was compounded by additional days on the market, a lower sale price, and ultimately a loss of profit.

The best way to tell if your property fits the *substandard finished project description before* you put it on the market is to ask the most anal retentive person you know to take a tour of the home. No doubt they'll point out every flaw.

Tip: Find the most finicky person you know, and have them do the final home inspection with you. That person will find every little flaw that may deter a sale.

Attention to Detail

You can't have everything. Where would you put it?

—Steven Wright

The rehab work on Cambridge Drive was complete. My project manager had the house cleaned, and it was ready to list for sale. So I packed a digital camera, staging items, water, and snacks into the back of my Tahoe for the one hour commute to Avondale, Arizona. On this trip, I would do my final walk through, stage the home, and take pictures to post on the MLS.

When I pulled up to the house, I noticed the trash bin on the curb. It was overflowing with construction debris. Inside, several of the doorstops were missing. The ones that were there were old and beat up. Both the family room and master bedroom had new ceiling fans. However, they were too small. Large rooms need at least 52" fans, and the ones installed were only 42" in diameter. The light above the kitchen sink and the garbage disposal didn't work either. The appliances were brand new but the cleaning crew left all the manufacturer's decals on them. The old microwave was left sitting in the garage. One of the garage doors wouldn't open. The back patio and side yard were filthy and in need of a good power washing.

All little stuff, I know, but sloppy nonetheless.

So how did my project manager miss all of these items? Here are a few theories:

1. He was in a hurry.

2. He thought I wouldn't notice them.

3. He didn't notice them.

My project manager has been on the job for over three years. He normally doesn't make this many mistakes on one property. He likely got in a hurry and didn't do his own final walk through before calling me to inspect the house. The bottom line is no one is going to have a better eye for the little stuff than you and the retail home buyer. Even the most thoughtful, experienced project managers and contractors miss stuff. It's human nature.

That's why it's so important you do a final walk through before putting the house on the market. Pay attention to detail and make sure everything is new, clean, and in its proper place before listing the property for sale. The psychological effect this has on the prospective buyer is twofold:

1. The home buyer will notice the flawlessness of the rehab.

2. The home buyer will feel you fixed it up properly because of the attention to detail.

Here's a checklist of some of the less obvious—but nonetheless important— items to inspect during your final walk through:

- Trash cans empty and placed on the side of the home or in the garage. (If they stink, dump some baking powder in them and store outside.)

- Lawn freshly mowed—shrubs trimmed—gravel fluffed.

- Yard free of construction debris, trash, cigarette butts.

- Front door and walk-up path clean.

- Make sure front door hardware is new or cleaned well to look like new.

- All interior and exterior windows are clean.

- All patios, sidewalks, decks and hard exterior surfaces are cleaned.

- If the home has a pool, make sure it's clean and leave any water features like fountains or waterfalls turned on during showing hours.

- Wall outlets and covers are new or cleaned well to look like new.

- Doorstops are new. (Don't cheap out here.)

- Smoke detectors aren't beeping. (This means their batteries are low.)

- Window blinds are open in the proper direction (vertical blinds).

- Make sure all light fixtures turn on and off.

- Set the clocks on the microwave, range, and anything else that requires programming.

- Haul away any old appliances or construction debris.

- Set thermostat to a comfortable temperature (not too hot or cold).

Remember, the goal is for the buyer to feel like they are walking into a brand new home. Even the little stuff must be done correctly for them to have this kind of experience.

Remember: Attention to detail matters. You want a potential buyer to walk into a house and just know immediately that the rehab job is of the highest quality.

Box Three: Sales

CHAPTER 11

Selling Your House

Every investor's goal should be to sell his or her fix-and-flip property for the highest possible price in the shortest possible time. Hopefully, you got a good deal when you acquired it and remodeled the home to match the features and finishes in the surrounding neighborhood. By doing so, you limit the problems that could come up once the house is ready for sale (like overpricing and underimproving).

Finding the Right Realtor (Listing Agent)

I'm a worried dad. My beautiful little girls are growing up too fast. They'll be dating soon, and I pray they make wise choices. I certainly don't want them hanging with the wrong crowd. So rather than leave this up to chance or divine intervention, I decided to start establishing some criteria for them. Their friends (the male kind) must be able to produce the following before a courtship can begin:

- A W-2
- A business plan
- Profit-and-loss statement
- Balance sheet

You may be saying to yourself, how many teenage boys can produce this kind of stuff? Very few, right? Exactly! With this criteria in place only the best and brightest will show up at my door on prom night. My girls will quickly weed out the unmotivated lazy slackers that have no idea what they want in life.

As a fix-and-flip real estate investor, I've discovered that setting high standards is also important when entering into a relationship with a Realtor. Now this may come as a surprise, but I am a Realtor. I chose to get licensed in 2007 because I wanted access to the Arizona Regional Multiple Listing Service (ARMLS). But just because I'm a Realtor doesn't mean I want to practice real estate. I'd rather pour hot coffee on my lap than deal directly with a retail buyer or seller.

■ **Tip:** Plan to work with Realtors, but be sure to set high standards for their services and relationship with you and your goals.

Realtors have their strengths and weaknesses. Some work well with buyers, others with sellers. Some have multiple years of experience; others are just getting started. None of this matters to me. Here's what I really want from a Realtor that represents me as the buyer:

- A great deal I couldn't find on my own.
- An honest, thorough assessment of the property's value.
- A ballpark figure for repairs and maintenance.
- Prompt offer preparation and submission to the seller.
- Proficiency with technology (zipForm, DocuSign, email).

Here's what I want from a Realtor that represents me as the seller:

- An honest, thorough assessment of the property's after-repair value (ARV).
- An honest, thorough assessment of the property's after-repair condition.
- A professionally written description of the property for the MLS.
- Professional photographs of the property for the MLS.
- Regular updates on showings.
- Retail buyer and buyer agent feedback on the property after showing.

- A professional opinion about the buyer's purchase offer (if the buyer's offer is good, great, or crap).

- A professional opinion about the buyer's mortgage lender or banker (if the buyer's lender seems smart and efficient or lazy and unmotivated).

- A friendly but aggressive negotiation with the buyer and the buyer's agent.

- The willingness to fight for me when it comes to price, repairs, appraisal, etc.

- The ability to efficiently navigate the transaction from the time the property goes on the market until a successful, on time closing.

These things are what make the Realtors I work with so, so valuable. One of my favorites, J.D. Manning, scours the MLS almost every day for bargains. When he finds one, I get an email with the property listing and recently closed comparables. This email also contains his estimate of repairs. If I agree with the valuation, he prepares the contract in zipForm (real estate forms software) and sends it to me in DocuSign (electronic signature software).

▓ **Tip:** Make sure you're working with a Realtor who uses electronic documentation and contracting software. It saves everyone lots of time.

J.D. and I recently purchased a distressed REO deal he found on the MLS. The rehab was finished in 7 days. On the 8th day, we put it on the market. 12 days later it went under contract. And 28 days later it closed for a $16,300 net profit. J.D. did his own final walkthrough at the property prior to listing it for sale and found a few minor things even I didn't see. He took high-quality pictures of the house and provided me constant feedback after it went live on the MLS. Once we got the offer from the buyer's agent, he sent me all the documents electronically so didn't have to screw around with scanners and fax machines (I can't believe people still use those things). Best of all, he checked up regularly on the buyer's agent and the mortgage lender to make sure the deal closed on time.

That makes J.D. the ultimate real estate investor's Realtor.

Whether you're looking for a contractor, attorney, accountant, Realtor, or love of your life, it's important to have minimum criteria in place.

And if you have a son that will be dating age in the next 7–10 years—he better start getting his financials together now. A dad like me will be reviewing them.

Just Say No to FSBO

I spent 15 years in the television news industry before I got into real estate investing. My first job was as a Chyron operator. The Chryon machine generated those graphics you see at the bottom of the TV screen. Eventually, I learned to operate the videotape machines and the teleprompter. By the time my career came to an end in 2002, I had done just about every job there was in the TV news business, from editor to producer to cameraman to live helicopter reporter.

After all those years schlepping camera gear around, I learned a funny thing about people—practically all of them think they're television experts. From my barber to my babysitter, I'd frequently hear criticism about news content, wardrobe, makeup, lighting, editing, and shot composition.

After careful reflection, I realized why this was so: most people own a TV and spend hundreds of hours a year watching it. This makes them television experts.

Occasionally, I'll run into a home seller or real estate investor hell bent on listing their property without the help of a Realtor. These home sellers think that because they own a house, or live in one, they are qualified to sell real estate. That's a big mistake.

So why would a homeowner go FSBO (for sale by owner)?

1. They don't want to pay a Realtor a huge commission for doing "very little" to "nothing."

2. They believe they can net more money without a Realtor.

3. They believe there is huge demand for their property, so hiring a Realtor isn't necessary.

4. Selling a home is easy. A Realtor isn't necessary.

You may recall I mentioned at the beginning of the chapter that I'm a Realtor. However, I rarely represent my company when it's buying or selling a property. Why? Because I believe that hiring a motivated, professional Realtor saves me time and makes me more money. A good Realtor will:

1. Market your property to a much broader base of homebuyers on the MLS, resulting in a higher sales price.

2. Prepare and follow through on the execution of the purchase contract, addenda, and required buyer and seller disclosures.

3. Negotiate more favorable terms for you.

4. Make sure escrow is opened and earnest money is deposited.

5. Use legal remedies to undo the contract and keep you out of court if the deal goes bad.

▓ **Remember:** If you think you can do a better job marketing your fix-and-flip property, take a cold shower and then think again. Besides, while the Realtor is selling your property, you can be out in the world finding another project.

Before continuing here, I'd like to further dispel a few myths associated with FSBO deals with a few truths:

Myth #1: A home seller can net more money because a commission doesn't have to be paid to a Realtor.

Truth #1: The savvy homebuyer will expect the home seller to "discount" the asking price by the amount of the commission because a Realtor isn't involved in the transaction, thereby negating any savings to the home seller.

Myth #2: A home seller can do a better job negotiating the sale of their property than a Realtor can.

Truth #2: A home seller's emotional attachment to the property makes rational negotiating nearly impossible and will blow up the deal.

Why do you think Hollywood actors, television personalities, authors, and athletes use agents to negotiate their contracts? It's because they know that hiring professional representation is key to getting a better deal. I suggest you do the same.

"It's Not an REO or Short Sale"

As the real estate market began to crash and burn in 2008, an interesting trend emerged. Housing stock became more segmented and experts started classifying the residential real estate market into three submarkets:

1. Normal sales (houses not in foreclosure or in need of some kind of bank approval to sell)

2. REOs—bank-owned houses

3. Short sales—homes owned by regular sellers that require bank approval to close (because the sale will likely result in a sum below the value of the homeowner's mortgage)

This segmentation wasn't necessary to understand the overall health of the real estate market prior to 2008, because nearly all sales that took place were normal sales. For example, in the greater Phoenix area more than 75% of all sales in 2008 were distressed sales (either REO or short sales).

Experts in this area also discovered during this time that there was a huge difference, on average, in sales price between normal sales, REO sales, and short sales. In some areas, normal sales were going for 20% or higher than comparable REO and short-sale properties.

How could this be? There are several reasons:

1. Normal sales are generally in better condition than REO and short-sale properties.

2. Normal home sellers can close more quickly than REO and short-sale properties.

3. Retail home buyers prefer to buy from individual homeowners because they can provide disclosures about the property (repairs, upgrades, improvements, etc.).

4. Retail home buyers prefer to buy from individual homeowners because they will usually agree to fix nonworking items found during inspections.

5. REO and short-sale properties must be purchased in "as is" condition, meaning the seller will make no repairs to the property.

When selling your fix-and-flip property, be sure to let the retail market know that your home is *not* an REO or short sale. This can be done best by your Realtor by writing it in the remarks section of the MLS. If you don't, your fix-and-flip may be unfairly stigmatized and sell more slowly and for a lower price than you want.

Promise a Quick Response and Quick Close

I'm all about instant gratification, which is why I hate ordering stuff online. I'm far too impatient to wait 3–5 business days for my goodies. I'd rather pay more to get what I want instantly at a retail store. My hunch is I'm not the only person out there that feels this way.

Imagine writing an offer on what is presumably the biggest purchase you'll ever make in your life and having to wait days, weeks, or months to find out if you're going to get it? How gut wrenching is that? That is precisely how a majority of homeowners in the post-boom era feel, because a bulk of the housing inventory is either owned by banks or require bank approval to sell. I've waited more than 60 days to close REO deals and over 6 months for short sales. This scenario puts a huge premium on normal sales because normal home sellers can respond quickly to purchase offers and can usually close in 30 days or less.

So in addition to letting the retail market know your fix-and-flip property is not an REO or short sale, also include language in the listing that states you will respond promptly to all offers and can close quickly.

▓ **Remember:** With so many distressed properties on the market, a promise of the ability to close quickly improves your chances of landing a successful deal significantly.

Staging

Martha Stewart is now under house arrest. So she'll go to her $40 million 153-acre estate. So she's going from the big house to an even bigger house.

— Jay Leno

T.J. Maxx. Target. Burlington Coat Factory. Walmart. Kirkland's. Goodwill. Did you notice I didn't mention Kmart? That's not because I don't buy these staging items at Kmart. It's just because there aren't many Kmarts around here. If I did, I'm certain some of the stuff would come from the Martha Stewart Living line.

What is "staging"? When you're done fixing your house, it'll be beautiful. But it'll be empty. And potential buyers want to buy a home, not an empty house. So to improve its chances on the market, I always add homey touches like a few pieces of furniture, plants, towels, and so forth. Think of the house as a movie set—you "stage" it so it looks (kind of) like a lived-in home.

And for what it's worth, I forgive Martha for the whole insider trader thing. She's paid her debt to society. But I still don't tune into her show—mostly because listening to her talk is about as exciting as watching a car rust.

So why else stage a vacant fix-and-flip property? Here are my top three reasons:

1.   A high percentage of buyers start their search for a home to buy online—a home that is staged looks more, well, homey.

2.   Staging items like pictures, rugs, towels, kitchen knickknacks, and plants gives the buyer an idea of how much space they will have in the house for their own stuff.

3.   Lived-in homes, or homes that looked lived in because they are staged, usually sell faster.

I like to stage the kitchen, master and hall bathroom, and master bedroom. The family room isn't a bad idea either. I use pictures, rugs, greenery like plants and trees, kitchen spice racks, canisters, and towels and any other knickknack kind of stuff that adds additional color to the house. The budget is around $500. I'm sure Martha Stewart would be proud.

Furniture

What about furniture when staging? It helps "identify the space." That's what my interior designer loves to say about furniture in vacant fix-and-flip houses. No doubt, a kitchen table, family room, and master bedroom set will help a potential home buyer picture their own stuff in the house. New homebuilders have been staging their properties with furniture for years, so it must be effective.

However, I don't generally use furniture in my properties. Here's why:

1.   It can be expensive to buy.

2.   It can be expensive to store when not in use.

3.   It's a pain in the butt to schedule drop off and pick up.

4.   It doesn't add any real value to the property.

The real benefit to using furniture is that it may help sell the property more quickly, which, by the way, is a huge benefit. It all boils down to how quickly properties are selling for in your market. If it's more of a buyer's market then putting furniture in the property may be the wise thing to do. If it's a seller's market you may want to skip the furniture.

Realtor Bonuses

Offering the buyer's Realtor a bonus to close by a specified date is an excellent way to get your fix and flip deal closed quickly. Sometimes all it takes is an extra $500–$1,000 to put your property on a buyer's agent's radar. Of course, Realtors shouldn't steer their customers towards a particular home.

And that's not what you're asking the agent to do. All you can hope the bonus does is get the Realtor to add your property to their list of homes to tour. If your asking price and rehab is right, then you might get an offer from an unexpected source.

Adding this incentive is simple to do. Your Realtor will include the bonus language in the MLS information sheet. There's a section that only other Realtors with access to the MLS can view.

Tip: Offer the buyer's real estate agent a bonus to find a qualified buyer and close the deal in the specified time. Since time is money, shortening the process is often worth the extra money you'll pay out for a fast deal.

Contract Analysis

This is an important topic. Let's waste no time.

The Top Five Most Important Contract Terms

Fixing and flipping is a roller coaster of emotion. However, the ultimate high, and unfortunately the most sickening of lows, will likely come when you receive a contract from a home buyer. Even after all these years of flipping, when I open up an email with an offer attachment for one of my properties, my heart begins to race. After reviewing it, I know I'm going to either party like a rock star or feel sick to my stomach.

Here are the top five contract terms I want to see as soon as I have the contract in hand:

1. Offer or purchase price
2. Buyer type: Cash or financing?
3. Closing date
4. Down payment
5. Earnest money deposit

Offer Price

Not all offers are equal. What does that mean? Just because you get two offers on your flip and one of the buyers is willing to pay more than the other for it doesn't automatically mean you accept the higher-priced contract.

Why?

How much home buyers are willing to pay for your property has little to do with whether or not they can actually close the deal. While the offer price is extremely important to consider when reviewing a purchase contract, it's only part of the equation. Equally important is the closing date, buyer type, type of financing, and down payment if the buyer is getting a loan.

I flipped a property recently that received four offers within a matter of hours of listing it for sale. Two of the four were for more than my list price and I didn't accept either of them. Both of those offers came from buyers that needed bank financing to purchase. Here's why I rejected them:

1. I knew the property wouldn't appraise for more than my list price.

2. Neither buyer had enough cash to make up the difference between the appraised value and their offer price.

The offer I accepted was for 5% less than my list price. The buyer paid cash and closed in two weeks. No appraisal was required and I got my cash two to three weeks sooner than waiting around for a bank-financed deal to close.

Tip: Believe it or not, sometimes it's wise to turn down a higher offer for your house.

Buyer Type: Cash or Financing?

Call me an infrequent flyer.

At the airport, you'll find me standing in the long line at the Phoenix Sky Harbor security checkpoint like a lamb being led to slaughter. The short line, the one that guys in fancy suits get to use, is strictly forbidden because I don't know the secret handshake. I also lack the preferred silver diamond elite status.

I board the plane with the Zone 5ers and pass by the first-class passengers as they sip their free booze and close multimillion dollar deals on their smartphones. Worse, these stuffy elitists refuse to make eye contact with me as I make my way to coach, where I go to suffer with the rest of the commoners for hours.

As I take my middle seat in row 27, it occurs to me that I'm a second class citizen of the air travel world—kind of like a home buyer using bank financing to purchase a property in the post-boom era.

In many parts of the country, it's a seller's market again. Inventory levels are stabilizing or slowly going down, and prices are inching up. Cash buyers account for 20%–40% of all sales in some states. And this new phenomenon has turned buyers that require home loans into the second-class citizens of the housing market.

Why?

Because real estate investors like me don't like selling to them. There are the three types of bank-financed buyers:

1. FHA (Federal Housing Administration)–approved home buyers

2. VA (Veterans Affairs)–approved home buyers

3. Conventional home buyers

I don't have time to get into all the technical differences between each of these types of borrowers and loan programs, but I will briefly explain how selling your property to each of them can affect the outcome of your deal.

FHA-approved Home buyers

FHA loan–approved buyers have very little, if any, cash to put down on their home purchase. In rapidly appreciating markets like Phoenix, it's difficult for appraisers to keep up with values. If you're a fix-and-flipper like me and are under contract with an FHA buyer, what happens if your house doesn't appraise for the offer price? You either lower it to match the appraised value or put the house back on the market. Neither option is very attractive.

If you're a fix-and-flipper and are under contract with an FHA buyer and the house does appraise, you're still not out of the woods. The FHA requires a second appraisal, usually ordered about five to seven days prior to closing. (At the time of this writing the second appraisal is required only *if* you've owned the property less than 90 days.) The FHA honors the lower of the two.

Then there's the inspection. The FHA has a laundry list of stuff that must be done in order for them to approve a buyer's loan. I once flipped a house to an FHA-approved buyer who didn't ask for any repairs. After the home inspection was complete, the FHA came back and required that I fix a bunch of stuff—to the tune of $1,500. Even worse, they had to send the inspector back at my expense to verify the items had been corrected, which pushed out the closing one week.

This is why many FHA borrowers are getting squeezed out of the market. They are the last people an investor wants to deal with. I know that price offers that overask likely won't appraise. The only way to get a deal done is to find a cash buyer or a conventional buyer with enough cash to cover the difference if the appraisal comes back low.

VA-approved Buyers

Buyers that qualify for VA financing must be U.S. service personnel or veterans. Like FHA buyers, few have the cash to put more than 3%–4% down on their home purchase. However, at the time of this writing, the VA does not normally require a second appraisal on flip deals owned for less than 90 days, nor do they have any strict guidelines for repairs. My experience selling to VA-approved buyers has been generally pretty good, although they can take up to 45 days to close because of all the extra red tape required by the lender.

■ **Tip:** Buyers with approved financing, like those who qualify for VA or FHA, are a good thing, right? Not always. Such loans come with strings attached, strings that can wreck your deal or your profit.

Conventional Home Buyers

Buyers obtaining conventional financing are typically required to put down 10%–20% of the purchase price by their lender. It's rare for the lender to require a second appraisal of the property or require the seller make any repairs in order to approve the loan. These loans typically take 30–40 days to close. The upside to selling a property to a conventional buyer is they usually have extra cash to make up the difference if the appraisal comes back too low.

For example, I flipped a property recently to a conventional home buyer putting 20% down for $125,000. Unfortunately, the property only appraised for $105,000. The buyer and I agreed to a new sales price of $118,000. Because there was still a $13,000 difference the buyer had to make up it up in cash—cash I knew the buyer could likely come up with.

Cash Buyers

As you've probably figured out, cash buyers are preferable to those who require bank financing. However, cash buyers sometimes expect huge discounts and make ridiculously low offers. They believe because they can close quickly and without bank approval you should give them a great deal.

I'll normally give a cash buyer a 3%–5% discount off my asking price, but no more. If I can't get that, then I'll wait it out for a buyer with traditional bank financing.

Of course, the only offer you may get may be from an FHA buyer. Don't worry. I've flipped dozens of properties to FHA-approved buyers and while the transactions didn't always go as planned, I still made money.

Note: Cash is king in fix-and-flip deals, but don't let cash buyers walk all over you. Give them a modest discount on the house, but don't give away the farm.

Closing Date

The faster you can close the sale of your fix-and-flip property the better. Even the most complicated FHA and VA deals shouldn't take more than 45 days. If they do, then you need to seriously consider cancelling and putting the house back on the market.

It's unwise to give the home buyer more than 30–40 days to close for four reasons:

1. It doesn't take that long to get a loan approved.

2. If you allow too much time, those involved in the transaction (the lender, the buyer's Realtor, the buyer) will get complacent, possibly extending the closing date even more.

3. The buyer may lose interest in the property.

4. Your holding costs will increase, and you could miss out on a great deal while waiting to close.

Down Payment

The bigger the down payment, the better—for two reasons:

1. If the home doesn't appraise for the contract price, the buyer with a sizeable down payment is more likely to have the cash to make up some or all of the difference.

2. Buyers with 10–20% down, or more, have a better chance of getting their loan approved (banks prefer to lend money to people with money) and the deal closed.

Earnest Money Deposit

The bigger the earnest money deposit, the better—for two reasons:

1. Buyers that put up sizeable earnest money deposits are usually serious about getting the deal done.

2. If the buyer elects to cancel the contract after the due diligence period has expired, you get to keep the earnest money deposit. (This varies state to state, so be sure to check in your area.)

It's customary in most real estate markets for the seller to receive 1% of the offer price as an earnest money deposit ($1,000 for a $100,000 offer price). However, an aggressive buyer that really wants the property will offer much more, usually 3%–5% of the contract price. As a flipper, these are the types of buyers I prefer because it means they are motivated to get a deal done.

▓ **Note:** Buyers who offer a large earnest money deposit are typically very motivated to see the deal go through.

Five Other Less Crucial but Still Important Contract Terms

Each of these offer terms and conditions may not seem very important, but for an investor they can add up quickly and reduce your bottom-line profit.

1. Closing costs

2. Title company

3. Home warranty

4. Homeowner's Association (HOA) fees

5. "As is" sale

Closing Costs

If you're working with a buyer that needs bank financing, it's likely they'll ask you to pay some or all of his loan costs. These include:

- Loan origination fees
- Homeowner's insurance
- Property taxes
- Title insurance policy (owner's coverage and lender's coverage)
- Title services (escrow fees)
- Document preparation fees
- Appraisal fee
- Pet relocation and maintenance fee (just kidding, but if the buyer could get you to legally pay for this then you can bet they would ask)

I've paid as much as $6,000 towards a buyer's closing costs and still made a handsome return. There's nothing wrong paying for this stuff as long as you have enough margin penciled into the deal. Remember, you can always negotiate for less. Don't be afraid to do so.

Title Company

Many title companies offer investors a discount, up to 35% off title and escrow fees. If the buyer chooses a title company with their offer, be sure you check to see if they will cut you a deal on these fees. If not, you can always counter the offer with a title company that will give you a discount.

Home Warranty

Retail home buyers are a skittish bunch. Understandably, there's a real fear of the unknown when purchasing a huge asset like a house. This is why most of them ask for you to buy a one-year home warranty. These range in price from $300 to $600. If a home buyer asks me to pay for all of their closing costs *and* a home warranty, I usually counter with this language:

"Seller to pay for up to 3% of buyer's closing costs. The home warranty shall be included in the 3%."

If the home buyer doesn't ask for any closing costs, I'll usually agree to pay for their home warranty.

Homeowner's Association Fees

In Arizona, most of the newer homes are located in subdivisions governed by a homeowner's association. These HOAs are charged with maintaining common areas and keeping homeowners compliant with the covenants, codes, and restrictions (CC&Rs). HOAs generate revenue by billing individual homeowners monthly or quarterly dues. They also line their pockets by charging fees to the principals in a home sale transaction. These costs have sophisticated, important titles like:

- Future improvement reserve
- Capital improvement fund
- Property transfer fee
- Disclosure fee

If your property is governed by an HOA and the home buyer asks you to pay for any or all of these items, then you better know for sure how much each will cost before you sign the purchase contract. I once paid over $2,000 in HOA fees after agreeing to cover these charges. Talk about a kick in the gut. Nowadays, I agree only to pay for charges incurred while I owned the property. Any costs associated with the purchase and sale of the property I split with the home buyer. And I make the buyer pay for any fancy dancy future improvement and capital costs. Why should I foot the bill for cool stuff I will never get to see or enjoy?

"As Is" Sale

One night I asked my nine-year-old daughter to go upstairs and get ready for bed. Her regular bedtime is 8:30 p.m. By 8:40 p.m., she still hadn't moved from her seat at the kitchen island. Evidently, she found the letter she was writing to her cousin more important than brushing her teeth.

So I asked her to get upstairs and get ready for bed again. And again at 8:45 p.m. At 8:50 p.m., again. By 9:00 p.m., I had to put my foot down. I got off the couch, paused the movie I was watching, and escorted her up to bed.

I guess asking my daughter to "get ready to go to bed" doesn't always mean "get ready to go to bed."

Negotiating with a retail home buyer is a lot like dealing with my daughter. I closed a flip deal last summer where the buyer agreed to purchase the home "as is." Now I don't know about you, but to me "as is" means "as is." No matter what the buyer and her inspector find wrong with the house—they agreed, in writing, to accept it in that condition.

But of course, that didn't prevent the buyer from asking me to fix things she found wrong with the house anyway. Nor did it stop her FHA lender from requiring certain items be fixed, per the loan underwriter. Here's what I found out had to be repaired, just two days prior to closing:

- Toilet won't flush properly
- Garage door missing sensors
- Roof certification required for all roof repairs
- Cracked window

So guess who is expected to make these repairs? The buyer's agent called my Realtor and asked us to take care of these items. I had to remind my agent that they agreed to purchase this home "as is." If the buyer wanted this stuff fixed, she'd need to call her own repairman and pay for it herself.

And that's exactly what the buyer did because she really wanted the house.

As the seller, I ordinarily would agree to repair any minor problems with a house. However, I make an exception with FHA buyers because as I explained earlier, FHA appraisers and underwriters are very particular.

I prefer to accept offers from buyers that are willing to purchase my properties "as is" because:

1. That means they must really be happy with the home's condition.

2. I save money by not having to make additional repairs.

Most of the time, "as is" sales work out splendidly for me.

That said, if you're selling a house to a buyer "as is" just remember the buyer may not take you literally. Get used to it. I have—in both my fix–and–flip business and at home with my daughter.

▨ **Remember:**   No matter what terms or conditions you offer buyers, they'll always want more. When you need to, put down your foot.

Clues from the Home Buyer and their Realtor

Never forget that when it comes to selling real estate, practically everything is negotiable. Don't be shy about countering on any or all of the terms listed above.

If the home buyer is motivated enough, they may offer to pay for all their closing costs and increase their earnest money and down payment. If you're fortunate enough to get multiple offers on your property, you can pit the buyers against each other to get more favorable terms and a higher price.

Here are some obvious clues that a home buyer really wants your house:

1. The buyer's Realtor tells you or your Realtor that the home buyer "really loves your house."

2. The buyer's Realtor tells you or your Realtor that "their buyer has just missed out on several other homes like yours to higher bidders."

3. The buyer's Realtor tells you or your Realtor that the house is located in the right school district.

4. The buyer's Realtor tells you or your Realtor that their buyer needs to find a home in the next 30–60 days.

5. The buyer's Realtor tells you or your Realtor that all the other homes they've looked at in the area really stink.

Knowing this information is extremely valuable. It puts you in a position of power. The home buyer will likely agree to any of your reasonable terms.

Of course, if your house has been sitting on the market for months and a decent offer finally comes along, you may want to accept it and be grateful to finally get it off the books. I've been there too.

Talking with Lenders

We've all heard about the Golden Rule. It's from the Bible. Matthew 7:12, to be exact. And it goes like this: "*So whatever you wish that men would do to you, do so to them; for this is the Law and the prophets.*"

But, in real estate we follow a different rule. It was first written in a 1971 *Wizard of Id* comic strip titled, "*Whoever has the gold makes the rules.*"[1]

Mortgage lenders have the gold so they make the rules. And since you'll likely be selling your flip property to a buyer that requires bank financing, it's wise to know the rules. It's also important you get to know the buyer's personal mortgage broker or lender to make sure they know the rules, too.

Do You Know This House Is a Flip?

In the good old days, if you could fog a mirror you could get a home loan. Demand increased, and prices skyrocketed. It wasn't uncommon for the same property to change hands three to six times in less than 90 days, each sale resulting in a 6%–10% increase in price. No doubt this helped lead to an artificial leap in prices in many markets throughout the country. A high-stakes game of musical chairs ensued. When the music finally stopped many unsuspecting retail home buyers (and investors) were left without a seat.

To put it mildly, after the market crashed in 2008, mortgage lenders tightened up their criteria.

---

[1] Johnny Parker and Brant Hart, *The Wizard of Id: Remember the Golden Rule!* (Fawcett Gold Medal, 1971).

These days, some lenders require the homeowner to hold title at least 90 days before they can resell the property for a profit. Other banks will allow a title transfer less than 90 days but require a second appraisal at the seller's expense. A few banks even limit how much profit a fix-and-flipper can earn on the sale. (I did a deal once where the bank forbid me from earning more than 20% profit of what I paid for the house until 120 days passed.) Needless to say, a brief conversation with the home buyer's lender prior to contract acceptance would have saved me time and thousands in profit.

Questions for Lenders

Here are some important questions you or your Realtor should ask the home buyer's lender about your property prior to contract acceptance:

1. Do you know that this property is a flip? (If the lender doesn't know the house is a flip from the beginning of the process, there will be problems as the closing date approaches. If the homeowner is getting an FHA loan, a second appraisal may be required. And if this isn't ordered by the lender soon enough, the closing could be delayed.)

2. Are there any restrictions on how long the seller has held title?

3. Are there any restrictions to how much profit the seller can earn?

4. If a second appraisal is required, when will it be ordered and who has to pay for it?

Besides the specific questions about your property, there is also general information about the transaction you'll want to know from the mortgage lender like:

1. Is the buyer well-qualified?

2. If the buyer is working with a mortgage broker, what bank is buying the loan?

3. What type of loan are the buyers qualified for?

4. Have you done many of these types of loans before?

5. Do you think this loan can close on time or close early?

6. Is there anything you see in the file that may delay the closing?

If your property is listed with a Realtor, then these are questions they should be asking the mortgage lender or broker. Sometimes lenders don't like to give out this information. A few may refuse to answer any of these questions.

However, you still need to ask. If the deal doesn't close on time, or at all, it's your money. If your Realtor refuses to ask these questions then do it yourself.

Why?

If the loan doesn't close, you don't get paid. The home buyer, her Realtor, your Realtor, and the mortgage lender must be put on notice that you'll be paying attention throughout the process. With this information in hand, you can hold others accountable if the deal doesn't get done on time.

Know the rules. And remember the golden rule. Both of them.

■ **Remember:**   If the loan doesn't close, you don't get paid. So don't just assume everything will "work out." Ask questions and get answers that will confirm—or refute—the buyer's credit-worthiness.

A Fix-and-Flipper's Best Friend

I've never owned a dog. It's not that I don't like dogs. It's just that I don't like picking up their poop. Sure, they're man's best friend and all. But if canines really cared about us that much, the least they could do is learn how to use the toilet. And bathe themselves.

I look for my best friends elsewhere. My best friend in the real estate world is a mortgage lender named Glen Reiley. He's a walking encyclopedia of knowledge, and I can count on him to inform me of the latest rule changes and loan underwriting hurdles facing fix-and-flippers like myself. The home loan ecosystem has changed since the crash and mortgage lenders are doing everything they can to cover their "ass-ets." I guess I can hardly blame them.

Rather than try to stay on top of all this stuff, I refer all my mortgage-related messes to Glen. And believe me, I get into my share of them.

Earlier this year, I accepted an offer from an FHA-approved buyer for a property located in Peoria, Arizona. This home buyer had chosen to work with a lender that was completely unqualified for the job. After two weeks, it became clear to me that the lazy lender would not be capable of getting the loan approved on time. I gave the home buyer an ultimatum—use my friend Glen Reiley to get this deal done on time or find another house to buy. Lucky for me, the home buyer agreed to use Glen, and the deal got done on time.

As you can see, having an experienced mortgage lender as a best friend is beneficial in two ways:

1. They can be counted on to help you understand the latest in mortgage finance rules and underwriting.

2. They can save your deals from going up in smoke.

So how do you make a mortgage lender your best friend? The same way you would a dog—you give them a treat.

Okay, not really. I realize I just insulted all the highly skilled and trained mortgage lenders in the world. Please, that was not my intent. A successful business partnership cannot be bought with a quick lunch at Chili's. It takes time. I'm all about win-win relationships. If you're serious about your business and are willing to refer business to a mortgage lender—the kind of treats they like best—then sending them three-flavored popcorn tins around the holidays won't be necessary (although it certainly won't hurt).

Tip: Part of successfully fixing and flipping properties is cultivating relationships that will ensure your projects move forward. Your best friends in the business should include one or two top notch mortgage lenders.

CHAPTER 14

Influencing Appraisals

As a real estate investor, every now and then I'm forced to play doctor and forensic pathologist, often in the same week. Admittedly, I'm not very good at either one. Not too long ago, I let a real estate deal flat line, and the cause of death still remains unclear. Fortunately, there is a lot that can be learned when you dissect a paper corpse. The writers of *CSI* could have never dreamed up an episode this good. Come to think of it, this story is actually more like a dark comedy than a murder mystery.

It Was a Beautiful, Sunny Day When . . .

It started out like any other normal real estate transaction. (Actually, it didn't. But isn't that how you begin any good script?) The subject property wasn't a short sale or REO but owned free and clear by my real estate partner and client. The subject property description: new carpet, paint, appliances, pool, blinds, ceiling fans, etc. Is this starting to sound like a police report yet?

The home goes under contract in six days to VA-qualified buyers, a very nice family currently renting in the area. The plot up to this point seems fairly predictable. The nice family buys the home of their dreams and lives happily ever after. Except that this is not Happily Ever After, Arizona—this is Buckeye, Arizona, where real estate market values have plummeted by more than 50% since 2008.

Of course, the trouble begins, as it often does, with the appraisal. Every good story needs a villain and in today's struggling real estate market, the lender fits the bill perfectly. And what made-for-TV villain would operate without a trusty accomplice? In this case, it's the appraiser.

So the contract price is $135,000. However, the appraisal comes back at $125,000. This is not an insurmountable price difference by any means. Luckily, my client/partner is a deal maker, not a deal breaker, so he lowers his price to $127,000 and the buyer agrees to bring an additional $2,000 to help make up the difference. Problem solved.

All's Well That Ends . . . Wait

Suddenly the bad guys don't seem so bad. My partner and I conclude the lender hired a competent, local appraiser that applied some common sense to the process. He carefully reviewed the subject property and three other comparable homes using similar criteria, but the appraisal came in a little low. It happens. Of course we are disappointed about it but the margins on this deal are still very good. So is it time for the nice family to ride off into the sunset?

Not so fast. Enter the next evildoer, Mr. Desk Review Appraiser. (Remember, he's a required in any VA loan.) This is starting to feel like a Batman and Robin movie . . . too many villains. And Mr. Desk Review Appraiser plays the part of the Joker. Let's look at a few lines from the script, I mean, the review appraisal.

It starts out on page three admitting that *"no physical inspection of the property has been made."* The madness continues on page six with the line, *"Reviewer's recommendation of value is based on this limited data and a complete appraisal should be completed on the subject if significant variances in value or descriptions of the subject physical characteristics are noted in this report."* And here's the Joker's punch line: *"Reviewer's recommendation: $93,000."* This is followed by the parting shot, *"Overall, the original appraisal report seems to be accurate and provides a fair estimate of value for the subject property."*

Huh? Never mind that the desk review appraiser is not licensed in the state of Arizona. Forget about the fact that the subject property or the comparables he used were never inspected or that he works 360 miles away in Sherman Oaks, California, and has no geographic competence. The lender used this desk review to trump the original appraisal and will only underwrite the loan based on the $93,000 value in the report, thus killing the deal.

And the Coroner's Report . . .

The autopsy results conclude that the lender did not really want to loan this family any money. A mortgage lender friend of mine pointed out there was probably something in the file the underwriter did not like. This desk review just gave the lender an excuse to bail out. Case closed.

How to Influence an Appraisal

In the aftermath of the housing crisis, Attorney General Andrew Cuomo of New York decided something must be done to keep the same thing from happening again. He pressured mortgage giants Fannie Mae and Freddie Mac to create an appraisal process free from the influence of mortgage lenders, Realtors, home buyers and home sellers.[1]

The HVCC Is Born . . . and Dies

Thus, in 2009 the Home Valuation Code of Conduct (HVCC) was born. Appraisal Management Companies (AMCs) were set up to act as intermediaries between the principals in the home sale transaction, buffering the individual appraiser from any external pressure. Mortgage lenders, Realtors, home buyers and home sellers were forbidden from having any direct contact with the appraiser. The FHA quickly adopted similar guidelines.

What followed was an unmitigated disaster. Because AMCs are, well, companies, their intent is to make a profit. They made money by adding their fee on top of what an appraiser would customarily charge a home buyer *and* by paying the appraiser less than they would customarily earn for said appraisal. Many of the most experienced appraisers left the industry and were replaced with unqualified, geographically incompetent hacks.

Real estate transactions like the one I just shared with you were blowing up all over the country because of bad appraisals. The recovery was stunted by years thanks to the HVCC.Appraisals:Home Valuation Code of Conduct (HVCC)

In 2010, the HVCC was shuttered when the Dodd-Frank Wall Street Reform and Consumer Protection Act was passed. However, AMCs are still being used today, and it's unlikely we'll see them go away anytime soon. This is why it's so important you understand how to legally influence appraisals.

---

[1] Richard Booth, "Appraisal Management Companies Create More Problems Than They Solve," American Banker, August 22, 2011, www.americanbanker.com/bankthink/AMC-appraisal-management-company-HVCC-Cuomo-quality-independant-1041437-1.html.

▨ **Note:** Like it or not, you will likely need to deal with AMCs and every once in a while, they may blow up your deal. Consider it a minor setback, and go out and sell that house to someone else.

And Now, the Four Methods

Of course, there's no guarantee any of the following four techniques will work for you, but here's my list:

1. Provide the appraiser a list of improvements you made to the property.

2. Provide the appraiser comparables in the area.

3. Meet the appraiser at your property and take the lockbox off the door so they can't enter unless you are there.

4. Leave a list of improvements and comparables somewhere in the home where the appraiser will find them.

But didn't I just tell you that home sellers are forbidden from having any contact with the appraiser? Well, yes, I did. This does not mean that the appraiser can't contact you or your Realtor. As a matter of fact, the appraiser must contact you or your Realtor before they can do their appraisal of the property *and* they will likely appraise your house at or near to the contract price if you follow these instructions.

First of all, the appraiser will likely call your Realtor to find out how to gain access to the property. The appraiser will also want to know if the power and water are on at the house. This is the perfect opportunity for your Realtor to ask the appraiser:

1. Do you know this house is a flip and the seller made significant improvements to the property?

2. Would it help if my seller provided you with a list of those improvements?

The appraiser will undoubtedly answer that they didn't know the house was a flip and say, "Yes, please provide me a list of improvements." At this point your Realtor will get the appraiser's email address. Your Realtor will then email the appraiser the list of improvements *and* comps that support your asking price. This is perfectly legal and works for me about eight out of ten times. And for what it's worth, I've never had an appraiser complain.

Just in case the appraiser doesn't call you or your Realtor, I suggest removing the lockbox from the property as soon as you accept the buyer's offer. If the appraiser shows up at the house they won't be able to get in. Then you or your Realtor can meet him or her at the house and provide the list of improvements and comps. If neither you nor your Realtor can be there to meet the appraiser, at least you can leave the list of comps and improvements in an obvious place where they appraiser will easily find them.

Tip: You *can* influence appraisers. Make sure they know how much you've improved the house, and help them out by finding comparables. Most of them won't take your efforts for anything but what they are—genuine help that will makes their lives easier.

Low Appraisals

I've never met a mortgage underwriter. Nor do I know someone who knows a mortgage underwriter. Maybe it's because they live below ground or in Siberia. Mortgage writers rarely appear in public. Some conspiracy theorists believe they live among themselves in the desert like the sand people from *Star Wars*.

If a mortgage underwriter is at a party and someone asks what they do for a living, the mortgage underwriter will likely respond, "I'm a bloodsucking vampire." After all, bloodsucking vampires are far more lovable than mortgage underwriters.

A mortgage underwriter's job is to verify the borrower can qualify for the loan. They analyze tax returns, bank statements, checkstubs, and debt-to-income ratios. Mortgage underwriters have also been known to ask borrowers for their retirement account statements, pet's name, family tree, and favorite color.

Don't get me wrong. It's not that mortgage underwriters are bad. It's just that they're evil. Or stupid.

So why do I feel this way? Here's an example, which falls into both the *evil* and *stupid* category:

> I sell a completely remodeled home to a conventional buyer for $200,000. The appraisal comes back at $192,000. The day after the appraisal was completed a home just like mine, three streets south, closes for $228,500. The appraiser is gracious enough to revise his report to include the sale. However, the mortgage underwriter refuses to allow the change and insists on using the lower value of $192,000. The deal blows up and a very nice family loses out on their dream home.
>
> I cancelled the contract and put the house back on the market. The next day I get another offer for $200,000. This time the appraisal comes back

at $200,000 because it includes the $228,500 comp. The deal closes 27 days later.

So, you see, the mortgage underwriter is evil. He uses a completely subjective process to crush the home buyer's soul (okay, that's a little melodramatic). But you have to admit, it's sad.

And the mortgage underwriter is stupid. Why on earth is the original appraisal carved in stone? Most appraisers agree that their appraisals are intended to support value, not to set value. So why not be reasonable Mr. Mortgage Underwriter and allow the revision?

Okay, maybe mortgage underwriters aren't really evil or stupid. Maybe it's the system they are required to follow.

So if you happen to be a mortgage underwriter, consider this a shout out. Rise up! Put down your pens, unplug your keyboards, and throw away your actuary tables. Walk away from the Dark Side. Join me in the fight against evil and stupidity?

Change the system. Let peace and common sense prevail. And may the force be with you.

Remember: Everyone involved in your fix-and-flip deal is a human being. And to err is human. Mortgage underwriters, it seems, err more than others. So be prepared to do some fancy footwork if the underwriter decides not to provide the homeowner with a mortgage based on the appraisal.

Four Options If Your Property Appraises for Less Than the Contract Price

All it takes is an appraiser that lacks geographic competence or a stubborn mortgage writer to torpedo your flip deal. If an appraiser's opinion of value comes in significantly lower than the purchase price you and the buyer agreed to, there is little hope for a simple resolution. Most appraisers are reluctant to adjust their value up, regardless of any supporting comps you or your Realtor provide, probably because it makes them look bad. And mortgage underwriters have a terrible habit of honoring the lowest appraisal submitted.

Once this happens here's what you can do:

1.   Ask the buyer to come up with cash to cover some or all of the difference between the appraised value and the contract price.

2. If you agreed to pay some or all of the buyer's closing costs then ask the buyer to pay them instead.

3. Ask the buyer to use a different lender. The new lender will then order a new appraisal.

4. Cancel the deal and remarket the property.

Cash to Cover the Difference

When a home buyer finds out that the house they want to buy is worth less than they offered, at least according to the real estate appraiser, an unfortunate event (for you) frequently occurs. Riddled with doubt, the home buyer backs out of the deal for fear of overpaying.

Unless you're flipping in a red-hot real estate market, few people are willing to bring extra money to the closing table to get a deal done. Instead, the home buyer will expect you to lower the purchase price to match the appraised value. And that really stinks.

Of course, you're under no obligation to drop the price. After all, if the home appraised for more than the contract price, you wouldn't expect the buyer to pay more right?

For deals that don't appraise at the value agreed upon, I generally ask the buyer to cover at least half of the difference. If the property received multiple offers, I may ask for the buyer to make up all the difference. You'll have to gauge the buyer's interest—and cash situation—to determine what solution will work best.

Lower Closing Costs

If you agreed to pay some or all of the closing costs, then another solution is to ask the buyer to pay these fees instead.

Let's say you're contractually obligated to pay 3% of a buyer's closing costs on a $200,000 purchase price. That's $6,000. However, the house appraises for $192,000. By getting the buyer to pay their own closing costs, you can make up all but $2,000 of the difference.

New Lender

Another option is to ask the buyer to use a different lender. A different lender will use a different appraiser that will hopefully value your property at or near the contract price.

But be careful using this technique if you're selling to an FHA-approved buyer. At the time of publication, all FHA appraisals are entered into a database and stick with the property for 6 months. If you decide to cancel the deal and put the house back on the market, you won't be able to sell to another FHA buyer because the old appraisal will still be in the system.

Cancellation

At the beginning of the chapter, I explained how I had to cancel the sale of a property. I had to put the house back on the market in order to sell it for my list price. Unfortunately, this may be your only option.

The bottom line is the appraisal process is very subjective. No two appraisers or underwriters will look at one property the same way. It's the world we fix-and-flippers live in. Be prepared to pull the plug swiftly if the appraisal comes in low.

Note: Mortgage underwriters will almost always hone in on the lowest appraisal, putting your deal at risk. There's always a way to solve your problem, but it could mean cancelling the deal.

Settlement Statements

The HUD-1 settlement statement provides the borrower and home seller with a breakdown of the costs and credits associated with the sale of the property, and it's used whenever the buyer is obtaining a mortgage.

The title or escrow company will provide a HUD-1 to both parties prior to closing for review. This is your chance to go over the numbers and make sure they all add up per the purchase contract. (See the appendix for a sample HUD-1.)

When I first started flipping houses I was intimidated by the HUD-1. All the numbers made my head hurt. Reading tea leaves seemed easier. However, I quickly learned that this document is the second most important document in the transaction, next to the purchase contract.

I highly recommend you go over the important sections below with your Realtor and the title company representative, sometimes known as an escrow agent or closing attorney (depending on your state), prior to the close of escrow. The escrow agent or closing attorney is a neutral third party that facilitates the sale between the buyer and seller.

▥ **Tip:** Don't be intimidated by the HUD-1. Or if you are, confront your fear and learn to read and understand it. As a last resort, find someone who understands it and can explain it to you.

Summary of Borrower's Transaction

Line 101 – This is the contract sales price (be sure it matches the price on the contract).

Line 103 – These are the settlement charges the borrower must pay, and they are broken down on the second page of the HUD-1.

Line 220 – This is the total amount paid by the borrower and includes the borrower's earnest money deposit, principal balance of new loan, funds to close, seller assistance, and taxes.

Line 303 – The total amount the borrower must bring to the closing.

Lines 801–811 – All of the loan costs the buyer must pay, including the origination charge, appraisal fees, etc.

Lines 901–905 – Prorated interest charges and homeowner's insurance.

Lines 1101–1113 – Title services, including title insurance, closing fees, owner's title insurance, lender's title insurance.

Lines 1201–1203 – Fees charged for recordation, transfer taxes, etc.

Summary of Seller's Transaction

Lines 406–412 – If you've paid taxes on the property ahead of time (through the closing date or beyond) you'll see a credit in these lines.

Lines 501–509 – This section lists the settlement charges to you, the payoff on your loan (if you have one), the owner's policy, and other loan charges you agreed to pay in the contract.

Line 603 – Probably the most important line for you—the amount you'll receive from the title company in the form of a check or wire transfer.

Lines 701–702 – The commissions you've agreed to pay your Realtor and the buyer's agent.

Lines 1201–1203 – In some areas you may be required to share any transfer taxes.

The bottom line here is you don't want to get stuck paying for something you didn't contractually agree to pay in the purchase contract. And you certainly don't want to overpay for something. The only way to verify this is to carefully audit the HUD-1 settlement statement. I've been investing in real estate for more than 10 years, and figuring out the HUD-1 still cooks my noodle from time to time.

Over the years, I've been fortunate to have attentive escrow agents and Realtors to check (and double check) the HUD-1 to make sure I didn't miss anything. If you're like me (math challenged), then get help with the HUD-1.

Common Mistakes in Selling

Since I started real estate investing in 2001, the flip on Cosmos Circle in Scottsdale, Arizona, reigns supreme as the winner of my biggest loser contest. This house would have tipped the scales at 450 lbs. and shed over 200 in the course of 90 days.

You remember that house with the barking dog I told you about in chapter three, right? I purchased it at a trustee's sale for $488,000, dumped $48,000 into it with upgrades that included brand new 20" travertine tile, carpet, stainless steel appliances, granite countertops in the kitchen and bathrooms, plantation shutters, light fixtures, plumbing fixtures and door hardware.

Things started out well. I had eight showings in the first four days on the market and received an offer for $572,500. However, my list price was $599,900. So I decided to reject the deal and wait.

Over the next 45 days I would get another 55 showings. Yes, that's right—55 showings! But, no offers. What was wrong with this house? Man's best friend next door, that's what was wrong with it.

You may recall I eventually sold Cosmos for $545,000 and it took almost 6 months to get off the books. After accounting for closing costs, commissions, and holding costs it was a net loss of $59,000. You can bet that since this nightmare ended, I stay away from homes in the higher price points. I've learned that the buyers in this range are just too picky.

I closed another property around this same time that backed to a busy street and had a large barking dog next door. After one day on the market, I got three offers, including one for $10,000 over my list price of $215,000. Evidently, buyers at this price point don't care about barking dogs. Or, maybe they know how to keep them quiet.

▌**Tip:** At least until you *really* know your market, stick with lower-priced properties. Buyers at the higher end are very picky and demanding, which can make it hard to fix-and-flip pricey homes profitably and in a reasonable amount of time.

The First Offer Is Often the Best Offer

Clearly, avoiding purchasing a property next door to a huge barking dog is a difficult mistake to avoid, especially when buying the house sight unseen at a foreclosure auction. No, I made the real mistake within four days of listing the house for sale. Over the years, I've discovered that most of the time the first offer I get is usually the best offer I'll ever get.

Why?

When a new home listing hits the MLS, home buyers and Realtors consider it warm and fresh, kind of like a hot loaf of bread taken straight from the oven. Interest in the property is at its peak during the first 7–14 days on the market. Most buyers and their Realtors recognize any offers on a new listing, especially a new listing that has been completely remodeled and is move-in ready, must be competitive. After all, the seller just put the house on the market, right? Why would he or she agree to give the potential buyer a steep discount so early on in the marketing process?

I should have jumped on the offer I got for $572,500. Sure, the net profit would have been considerably less than I expected but at least it would have been a profit. My gut told me to accept the offer, but I couldn't convince my brain to pull the trigger.

▌**Remember:** The first offer you get is often the best one you'll get. Dismiss it at your peril.

Waiting for a higher offer really cost me in both holding and opportunity costs. Your real estate market is probably different than mine, so it may take longer to flip a house. Regardless, the theory is the same. The longer a house sits on the market, the staler it becomes to the retail buying public. The perception is there is something "wrong" with the property.

And Then There Are These Mistakes

Here are three more common mistakes that could cost you when selling a property:

1. Giving the buyer extra time to close.

2. Allowing the buyer to move in prior to close of escrow.

3. Renting the house out because you can't sell it for a profit.

Giving the Buyer Extra Time to Close

There are usually seven people involved in the closing of a real estate transaction:

1. The home seller (you)

2. The home buyer

3. Your Realtor

4. The buyer's Realtor

5. The appraiser

6. The buyer's lender

7. The escrow officer, attorney, or both depending on your state

Within the course of 30–40 days, all of these people must coordinate the exchange of information so that the deal can close on time. Flip enough houses and you'll quickly find out how easy it is for someone along the way to drop the ball, thus delaying the closing date. And the person with the most to lose when this happens is the home seller (you).

When the home buyer, their Realtor, or their lender asks for a closing date extension it's because one of them screwed up. Their mistake could easily cost you hundreds, if not thousands of dollars.

I generally won't grant the home buyer any additional time unless they put some skin in the game. I'll write an addendum to the contract demanding the buyer's earnest money be released to me immediately. Furthermore, it's nonrefundable if the deal doesn't close. If the home buyer signs the addendum, then I can be sure that closing will occur. In the event it doesn't close, at least I get to keep the buyer's earnest money deposit, which may cover some of my holding costs. If the home buyer refuses to sign the addendum, then I know the deal was probably going to fall through anyway and I can start remarketing the property immediately.

Allowing the Buyer to Move In Prior to Closing

Let's say, for reasons beyond anyone's control, the closing of your flip deal gets delayed by two weeks. The homebuyer is parked in front of your property with a moving van packed with all their stuff. They just finished driving over 2,000 miles to get there. Their lender promised the deal would get done today. Now they're on the phone with your Realtor, begging for permission to move in prior to the closing date.

What do you do? It's not the buyer's fault, right? Why should they have to suffer?

This may sound cruel, but you cannot, under any circumstance, allow the buyer to move in. There's no significant financial benefit to letting them take prepossession of the property, and there's significant potential for financial disaster if the deal doesn't work out. It's a high-risk, low-reward scenario.

Imagine if, two weeks after moving in, the buyer's loan is denied. Now what?

You're no longer a fix-and-flip investor—you're a landlord with a very disgruntled tenant. Even if you had the home buyer sign a short-term lease agreement prior to move-in you'll still need to go through some sort of eviction process the get them legally removed from the property. And what happens if someone is injured on the property during this time? You, the owner, may be liable for any legal or medical expenses.

In the past, I have allowed the home buyer to put their stuff in the garage prior to closing if I'm absolutely certain the deal is going to get done. If you choose to do this, be sure to have the buyer sign a release that says if anything happens to their belongings (damage, theft, fire) they'll hold you harmless.

Don't worry about the home buyer. There are lots of options available if they can't move in. More than likely, there are friends and family that can help them out. Or, better yet, they can stay in an extended stay hotel that offers free continental breakfast with those fantastic Belgian waffle makers. Yum.

Tip: Never allow someone to move into your house before the deal has closed. Never.

Renting Out the House Because It Won't Sell for a Profit

Electing to lease out a house because you can't sell it for a profit is a big mistake, unless acquiring rental properties is part of your overall plan to build wealth through real estate (and you have plenty of cash/credit to do other flip deals). I once took a $12,000 loss on a house and then, with the same capital, turned around on the very next deal and netted a $31,000 profit. What would have happened if I chose to rent out that property instead? My cash would have been tied up in a bad deal and the loss would have been compounded with missed opportunity costs.

There's no problem that lowering the price can't fix. Unload that bad deal and move on to the next profitable opportunity.

Note: Not every deal will work out. Every so often, you'll lose money despite your best efforts. Knowing that in advance somehow makes it easier to soldier on and ensure that your efforts will reward you in the long term.

Box Four: Raising Capital

18

Creating a Track Record

The home was empty. You know that look, right? There was a pile of old phone books on the porch. A flyer for a housekeeper, landscaper, and pool cleaner were dangling on the front door knob. I peeked over the side gate and could see the pool had been drained. The plaster was peeling off the sides.

Sure, you can drive through just about any neighborhood in the post-boom era and find vacant houses. But this was 2005. The underlying mortgage on the home was only $77,000—the market value $200,000. Why was this house abandoned? Why hadn't the owner sold it? She could have easily flipped it to an investor like me for $100,000.

With the few clicks of a mouse and a quick phone call I had my answer. The owner, who was now living in Hebron, Indiana, could not sell the house and make a profit. The Arizona Attorney General's office had made sure of that. They recorded a $125,000 lien against her back in 1993.

I made another quick phone call to the AG's office and found out they'd be willing to release the lien for $25,000. Problem solved. With the lien released I could buy the house and give the owner a little cash too.

Unfortunately, time was not on my side. The home was scheduled for auction the next day. My only option was to fly out there and get the notarized deed and closing documents directly from the owner. The closest airport was Chicago O'Hare. I rented a car and met her in Hebron at a Holiday Inn Express just off the interstate.

I arrived back in Phoenix the following morning (the auction was at 2:00 p.m.)—paid off the loan, and recorded the deed. Boy, was that close.

I have lots of stories like this from the preboom era. I was just starting out in real estate back then, working for a local investor in a mentor/protégé relationship. He would travel to any zip code to put a deal together if it made him money. What I'd discover later is that I could parlay these stories into a business of my own. I was slowly developing a track record.

Around this same time, my father-in-law, a retired IBM manager and successful real estate investor, came to Arizona from New York for a visit. He was curious why I wasn't doing this real estate investing thing on my own. I explained that I lacked the financial resources. After analyzing the numbers on a few of my previous deals he decided to loan us some "love" money.

Of course, the numbers I provided made sense to my father-in-law. But let's face it—he was really investing out of love (presumably for my wife, not me).

I've found that's how most entrepreneurs get their start. A family member or friend will believe in you enough to front some cash. If you make them money, they'll invest more. And better yet, they'll tell other friends and family about your business. Sooner or later they'll want a piece of the action, too.

However, none of this happens without a track record. Back then I used a simple Excel spreadsheet to track the numbers. These days, it's QuickBooks with profit and loss statements and a balance sheet. If a potential investor considers coming on board I send them to a password protected area of my website that has an up-to-date financial pro forma.

A fancy business plan and high-quality website aren't enough—you need a track record to raise private capital for buying real estate.

As for that vacant house I bought back in 2005—I called one of our wholesale buyers to tell him about it just before I boarded in Chicago. When I landed I had a voicemail from him. He agreed to pay our asking price of $125,000.

I told the story of my last 24 hours with the man sitting next to me on the plane ride back to Phoenix that day. He asked if I was a real estate investor. No, I said. But I did stay at a Holiday Inn Express last night.

Tip: Having a fancy web site and an immaculate business plan aren't enough to attract capital. Nothing beats successful experience for finding investors and building a business.

Rebuilding a Broken Track Record

As I mentioned at the beginning of the book, life was good for me prior to the real estate market crash in 2008. I drove a fancy car and wore expensive clothes. I even belonged to a stuffy country club, though I didn't play much golf. I was managing over $2 million of private investment capital. I was unstoppable.

Then all hell broke loose at the end of 2007. My $16 million real estate empire disappeared practically overnight. Every dollar I raised and all the goodwill I'd built with my investors evaporated. The party was over.

That's why meeting my mentor, Keith, in 2009 was such a blessing. After working with him for less than three months, a friend and former business colleague, Manny Romero, called me out of the blue. He'd been on the road traveling for business the past year and was getting sick of living out of a suitcase. I explained to Manny how Keith and I met and that I was working for him as a project manager and Realtor. I also shared the four boxes concept with him. Manny was impressed so I showed him several of the properties Keith and I were working on. Afterwards, he popped the question, "Marty, could we partner together and do these kinds of deals?"

Of course, I said yes.

Using Keith's system and $180,000 Manny rose one month later, we started investing in real estate again. Since July of 2009 Manny and I have flipped over 80 houses and captured over $1,000,000 in new investment capital.

In 2011, I finally turned the corner financially. Although these days I drive a used Infiniti with 110,000 miles, I don't wear a Rolex watch anymore, and I shop at T.J. Maxx, Ross, and Kohl's. I ate a big piece of humble pie in 2008, and I don't ever want to taste it again. But, believe it or not, I'm grateful for being knocked down. It forced me to check my ego at the door.

How to Get Started

If you lack the funding necessary to get started fixing and flipping houses then here's how to get your business off the ground:

1. Leverage the success of a mentor/partner/client.

2. Raise your own capital.

3. Build your own business.

4. Attract new investors/working capital.

Let's look at each one in turn.

Leverage the Success of a Mentor/Partner/Client

Would you let someone with no formal training or experience fill a cavity in your tooth? Or work on your broken-down car? I'd be willing to bet you wouldn't let someone cut your hair unless they had done it before. So how can you expect someone to invest money with you or loan you money to flip a house if you've never done it?

I got a first—and second—start in real estate investing with the help of a mentor. I didn't realize it at the time, but I was creating a track record for myself by working along side two accomplished real estate investors.

Remember: To attract investors, most of all you need credibility. That means building a resume in the real estate industry.

Keep in mind, neither of them were gurus. You know the type, right? You've probably seen them on late night infomercials or heard their ads on the radio. These carnival-barking frauds promise big results for little effort. When you show up at their free real estate investment seminar they give you a minuscule amount of information and then attempt to upsell you on a $2,997 weekend foreclosure boot camp where you'll get the exclusive super secret inside investor information.

These guys aren't mentors—they're salesmen who are likely trying to make enough cash off of their seminars to do their own real estate deals.

A real mentor won't charge you a dime for what they know. They'll share their knowledge of the market and industry if you can help them in return. The relationship must be a win-win.

Take my friend Keith, for example. He brought me on board and taught me the four boxes concept because I helped him—first as a project manager and later as a Realtor. I was willing to do whatever it took to relearn the business—from driving 50 miles across town one way, to mopping floors and scrubbing toilets. No task was too menial because I recognized his knowledge was valuable. Keith saw how much I was willing to do so he was happy to share his expertise with me. Together we both prospered. And less than three months later, I found a business partner with access to $180,000 in investment capital.

Things may not progress this quickly for you. First of all, it will take time to find a mentor. Once you do you'll have to convince him or her that you can bring something to the table. The two most valuable things to a fix-and-flipper are money and deals—more money to do more deals and more deals to make more money. If you can provide one or the other—or both—then there's some real potential for a mentor/protégé relationship to develop. However, you must be willing to prove you're worth the effort and be willing to accept the most mundane tasks from your mentor with grace, humility, and enthusiasm.

Even after you begin working with a mentor, it could be a year or more before you raise that first dollar. I quit my job as a television news cameraman in September 2002 to start real estate investing full-time. After stumbling around in the dark for two years, I finally found an investor (my father-in-law) willing to fund my first flip deal.

LEGAL DISCLAIMER

The U.S. Securities and Exchange Commission (SEC) forbids any general solicitation of investment opportunities. This means you can't advertise on the TV, the radio, in print media, or the Internet. You must have a substantive relationship with the investor prior to receiving any investment capital.[1]

Raise Your Own Capital

Obviously, I had a "substantive relationship" with my father-in-law before he started investing money in my fix-and-flip business. But how did I raise the rest of the money?

Just like almost all start-up businesses do it—word of mouth. It's another reason why creating a track record is so important.

Those around you—your friends, family, colleagues, and business associates—will see and hear about your success in fixing and flipping real estate and may want to become involved. I'm sure that when I left a very stable job in the television news industry, my loved ones worried. But after two years of surviving, and eventually thriving, it became clear that I wouldn't end up living in a cardboard box on the side of the road. I slowly became someone successful that people wanted to invest their money with.

Once the crash was over I quickly reestablished a track record of success, and the money began flowing in again. It all started with Manny, my business partner. He knew an investor that had $180,000 in a self-directed IRA, and in July 2009 we were able to use it to flip two houses. However, it would be about six months before either of us could give up our other commitments to focus on the fix-and-flip business full-time.

---

[1] http://www.sec.gov/answers/rule506.htm.

With the working capital Manny and I had, we could flip about 10–12 houses a year. Our average net profit was $10,000. However, we had to split that with our investor partner. After all the numbers were crunched we could expect to annually take home about $25,000–$30,000 each.

Needless to say, that wasn't enough cash for me to quit working for Keith or for Manny to give up his traveling sales job. But this phase is a necessary step to build experience and begin creating a track record of your own deals.

Build Your Own Business

The big breakthrough for us came at the beginning of 2010. After successfully flipping eight properties in the second half of 2009, several of our friends, family, and past business associates started taking notice. It started with a $40,000 investment in January. By the spring we raised another $200,000.

Manny was finally able to quit his job (and unpack his suitcase). I had to sit down with Keith and explain to him why I couldn't be his project manager and Realtor anymore.

It was a defining moment for both of us. Just a year prior we sat together sipping coffee and swapping real estate horror stories, lamenting our empty bank accounts, and praying for the wisdom to make wiser choices in the future. Now we were meeting under much different circumstances. His business was booming and mine was getting ready for takeoff.

I thanked Keith and told him how grateful I was for the opportunity to serve him and his partners. He wished me well and offered his advice and expertise moving forward. Since parting ways back then, we continue to talk on the phone and meet for lunch regularly. We also collaborate on deals from time to time. The relationship is still a win-win.

Tip: Maintain good relations with everyone you work with in the business. You want them to continue thinking of you as a potential partner.

Attract New Investors/Working Capital

You've probably heard the expression "success breeds success." No matter how you get the money to fix and flip a property, whether it's your own or someone else's, done profitably you'll attract new investor partners and additional working capital. It's inevitable.

Why?

The perception is that fixing and flipping houses is sexy. Hopefully by now you've learned that it's not. Fixing and flipping houses is difficult. There are a lot of moving parts. Many financially savvy people lack the time required to learn the business. However, they have the cash to invest. They'd much rather give it to an experienced operator that has the technical skills, system, and team already in place. That someone is you.

With a track record and solid financial records you'll never lack the capital to acquire, rehab and sell distressed real estate.

Where Is the Money?

Because the U.S. Securities and Exchange Commission (SEC) strictly forbids the general solicitation of investment capital, you'll need to be creative in getting the message out about your fix-and-flip opportunity. Remember, a substantive relationship is required with an investor or partner.

How substantive? The SEC is vague in their description. I took a class once on private-equity fundraising, and the instructor told us that if we meet the prospective investor at a back yard barbeque, bar, camping trip, or networking event then we were probably legal in eyes of the SEC.

The rules aren't as clear if you borrow money from an individual to invest in real estate. In this scenario the investor is a lender.

Be sure to check the laws in your state and consult with an attorney before taking in other people's money to do a real estate deal.

Now, with that out of the way, let's talk about the three ways my partner and I have raised money legally:

1. Through our warm market.
2. By attending networking events.
3. By using social networking.

Important: It's essential that you talk to an attorney before you start raising capital. You need to fully understand what you're getting into and what you can and cannot do when it comes to soliciting funds.

Warm Market

The people you know—that's your warm market. Prior to the boom, just about everyone I ran into wanted to know about my business. After I had a knee surgery done in 2005, for example, my orthopedic surgeon invested $100,000 with my company.

In the beginning, Manny and I got investment capital from friends and family. This is what I call "love" money. They were willing to take a chance with the limited track record because of trust and goodwill.

However, I don't recommend you go around bragging about all of your real estate investment success to your friends, family, and business associates hoping they'll scratch you a check for $50,000. Instead, wait to be asked about your business and then subtly explain how much more profitable it could be with additional capital. Even if no one in your warm market is interested, they may know someone who is.

■ **Tip:**   The easiest money is going to come from people you know. And not just relatives and friends but also from business associates, professional people like your doctor or accountant, and friends of friends.

Networking Events

I'm not talking about referral generation meetings over breakfast where each participant stands up and gives their 60-second elevator speech. Then everyone passes around his or her business card.

No, I'm talking about those networking events where the participants may have discretionary income to invest in real estate. Here are a few examples:

1.   Political mixers.

2.   Wine tasting clubs.

3.   Running or biking clubs.

If asked what you do when attending these events, reply, "I own and manage a real estate investment business." This will undoubtedly spark interest. (Hint: be sure to ask what they do, too, and ask lots of questions.)

My business partner Manny is the master of networking events. He belongs to several clubs, personal development organizations, and mastermind groups. His selfish reason for attending these events is to tap into other peoples' networks. Manny does very little talking and a lot of listening. It's a brilliant strategy that has netted us over $250,000 in investment capital.

■ **Tip:**   Network at organizations that attract people with money—arts groups, certain charities, clubs, etc. With it harder and harder to profit from traditional investments (like stocks and bonds), there are more people than you realize looking for a place to invest excess cash.

Social Media Networking

Chances are that you have a mom, dad, grandma, grandpa, sister, brother, aunt, uncle, friend, coworker, or business colleague that completely rejects the notion that social networking is valuable and can somehow, either directly or indirectly, improve their lives and the lives of others. Maybe you feel this way too.

This little section is about them. And you, if you're among the last of the social media holdouts.

I know a guy that owns a home remodeling business. His craftsmanship is exemplary, yet his company is struggling to make ends meet. Still, he won't take the time to learn how to set up a blog with before-and-after pictures of his remodeling projects. To me, this is the equivalent of him not knowing how to use a hammer.

One buddy sends me six to ten chain emails a day, addressed to 15 other people on his contact list. This person won't get on Facebook because "it's a waste of time." I have another family member that won't do any social media because she is afraid her identity will be stolen.

Clearly, the social media holdouts have their reasons for not going online. However, I believe the benefits far outweigh the negatives. Since the real estate market crash I've used social media (my blog, Facebook, Twitter) in my business to:

- Get a publishing deal to write this book.
- Raise over $200,000 in investment capital.
- Connect directly with journalists at the *L.A. Times* and *Wall Street Journal*.
- Refer home buyer and seller leads to my Realtor partners.
- Refer home remodeling work to my contractor partners.

On a personal level, social media has helped me to stay in touch with old friends and distant family. Recently, a soccer buddy sent me a message on Facebook to see if I wanted to join his indoor team. He also asked me to list his house for sale. That's a valuable connection that probably wouldn't have been made in the offline world.

Technology can be frightening and new technology, even more so. While I'm fairly certain lots of people initially debated the value of the automobile, the airplane, the computer, the Internet, cell phones, email, and text messaging, few would disagree that today they all help to improve our lives.

So the next time a social media holdout you know wants to bash the medium, bookmark this section of the book and make them read it.

Below is a list of the social media I use (and how I use them) to build business contacts and raise capital legally:

- **My Blog** (flippingphoenixhouses.com). This is the nerve center of my social media campaign. All of my other social media endeavors funnel directly to my blog. Here I write posts three to eight times a month, mostly about current projects but also about trends in the Phoenix market and other local housing news. I also post instructional videos here about auction bidding, staging, and rehabbing. My willingness to share all of this education for free keeps my email inbox full and phone ringing with potential investor prospects. (*Note:* Nowhere on my site do I advertise investment opportunities. My blog is strictly educational.)

- **BiggerPockets.com Real Estate News Blog** (bigger pockets.com/renewsblog.com). BiggerPockets.com is an online real estate investment community with over 100,000 members. The site includes a real estate news blog, and I'm a weekly contributor. My articles are seen and read by thousands of people. Of course, there's a link on BiggerPockets.com back to my blog. This site, like mine, is also free. I actually get more exposure through BiggerPockets.com than I do with my company blog. Aspiring real estate investors, prospective investors, and even news reporters contact me for additional information about fixing and flipping and market recon.

- **Facebook.** I use Facebook to tell stories about my business. I'll frequently put the posts I write on my timeline, which link back to my blog. I also put these articles in the various real estate investment groups I belong to on Facebook.

- **Twitter.** I use Twitter as a branding tool. I follow all the movers and shakers in the real estate industry and post my insight on the market in 140 characters or less. I also tweet out links to my blog posts. Using this medium, I've made contacts at the *Wall Street Journal* and the *L.A. Times*. Let's face it, I would have never met these reporters in the offline world so, yes, Twitter is valuable.

- **YouTube Videos.** My YouTube channel (youtube.com/ FlippinPhoenixHouses) serves two purposes: It hosts the videos that I embed into my blog, and it provides additional search engine pop. Off all the social mediums I use, YouTube gives me the most reach distance-wise. I recently spoke to a prospective investor from Dehli, India, that found my videos on YouTube. He was so excited when we spoke on the phone that he said it felt like he was talking to a celebrity. Good stuff.

My favorite social networking success story involves a 24-year old defense contractor in Iraq. This guy watched my YouTube videos and read my blog for over a year before finally reaching out to me via email. He asked if I ever partner with investors on my fix-and-flip deals.

We arranged series of calls on Skype, and he eventually invested $35,000. To this day we've never met face to face. The entire business relationship was created and consummated via social networking.

Putting It All Together

To truly take your business to the next level you'll need to incorporate all three of these strategies. I tell people that my fix-and-flip business is like a nonprofit organization (constantly in fund raising mode).

Why? Life happens.

Investors come and go. Even if you provide them with above-average returns, eventually they'll need to get their money back. You've got to keep the investor pipeline full or you won't have the necessary cash to meet your investment goals.

Remember: No matter what stage your business is in, you'll need more cash to take it to the next level. It's rare to be able to generate enough capital solely from your operations, so a neverending part of your job is to find new investors.

CHAPTER 20

Types of Investors

Everyone has a junk drawer. It contains pens, pencils, paper clips, AA batteries, loose change, and TV remotes. And if you're like me and have daughters it also has pink hair clips, Barbie doll accessories, and Peter Piper Pizza game tokens. I love my junk drawer, a household melting pot of stuff, a place for everything I don't have a drawer for.

What does this have to do with investor types? I have met many newbie, would-be, so-called, part-time, full-time, and, yes, even sophisticated investors that use this junk drawer mentality to invest in real property. At a networking event, I met a guy who was hocking developable land in Mexico one second and a wholesale flip-opportunity in suburban Phoenix the next. Then there's the guy I know who is running a short-sale business here in Arizona but is also trying to buy a property in California that he can convert to an assisted living home.

You've heard the phrase "jack of all trades but master of none"? That is the definition of a junk drawer real estate investor. If you're going to have sustained, long-term success in real estate you must be very clear and consistent and expect the same from the investors you choose to partner with. Before you take a dime of someone else's money, be sure to determine if they:

- Seek an equity position or debt position in the deal.

- Want to be actively involved or passively involved in the deal.

Tip: Just as you want to become an expert in a certain slice of the real estate market, you'll want investors who can remain focused on your business, your goals, and your opportunities. Unless they are truly passive investors, avoid dabblers.

Equity vs. Debt Partner

An equity partner will want a piece of the action. In other words, they will desire a percentage of the profit from the flip deal. Equity partners recognize that the upside profit potential will provide a far greater return than a set interest rate. They also realize—or most do anyway—that they can lose money in a project. (Probably best to avoid anyone who doesn't understand the downsides to real estate investing.)

Debt partners are lenders. They will lend you money to flip a property for a set interest rate. These debt partners are sometimes referred to as private money or hard money lenders.

There are pros and cons to working with equity and debt partners. If you choose to do business with an equity partner and the deal goes badly, at least you're not on the hook for any big interest payments. However, if the flip makes a huge profit, you give a lot of it up. With a debt partner you keep most of the profit, minus the interest payments. On the other hand, you're paying that interest even if you lose money on the deal.

In the following two chapters I'll discuss how to structure deals with equity and debt partners.

Active vs. Passive Investor

An active investor is directly involved in the day-to-day operation of the business. In a flip model, for example, that means identifying the subject property (via the MLS, wholesalers), doing the due diligence (market analysis), arranging the financing, acquiring and rehabbing the home, marketing and finally selling it on the retail market. There's also a lot of coordination involved throughout the process, like dealing with utility companies, insurance agents, construction trades, loan officers, title companies, sellers, buyers, and buyer's agents.

The passive investor funds the deal either with traditional bank financing, a secured/unsecured promissory note, or partnership interest in the entity that is created by the active investor to purchase and sell the properties. It is then the responsibility of the passive investor to get out of the way and collect the profit, also known as mailbox money.

Keep in mind you can be both in any real estate deal and most investors are, especially when just starting out. As you become more successful, more often than not, you'll meet active real estate investors disguised as passive real estate investors. They will tell you that they want to invest money with you. But before long they want to be involved in every decision, no matter how trivial. There is an affectionate term for this type of investor: the PITA, or the pain in the ass investor. Needless to say, stay away from a PITA.

▓ **Note:** There's nothing worse than a PITA investor. You'll spend more time tending to their needs and requests and educating them than is worth it.

Managing Expectations

My loveable grandpa, Leroy Martin Boardman, went by the nickname "Gabby." It was bestowed upon him because of his remarkable gift for gab. Grandpa Boardman would opine, debate, discuss, and pontificate with anyone in earshot. His pulpit was a counter stool at the Beacon Diner in downtown Belvidere, Illinois, population 23,000. The men who would gather there for morning eggs, toast, and coffee were subjected to my grandfather's talks on politics, business, religion, farming, and family. On Sundays, he hung out at Ike's Cigar Store where he'd play pinochle and take the opposite point of view in every conversation. He would argue just for the sake of arguing.

I share my Grandpa Boardman's insatiable desire to communicate and debate with the masses. It's in my DNA. But over the years I've learned the hard way that in business and personal relationships, success is not achieved by talking. History demonstrates that the great ones, from Jesus to Benjamin Franklin to Abraham Lincoln, were all extraordinary listeners.

This is why I've spent the last 4 years training myself to shut up. No one ever learns, or earns much, by talking or arguing.

To begin the process, I bought Dale Carnegie's *How to Win Friends and Influence People* on audio CD. I listened to it in my car and on my iPod, over and over and over again. Since 2008, I've heard it about a dozen times. Still, genetics are very hard to overcome. Sometimes my instincts take over and it's blah, blah, blah, blah, and more blah.

So whenever I get the urge to debate, interrupt, or generally just talk for the sake of talking, I pop one of Dale Carnegie's CDs in my car and listen to the entire book—again. The results that follow are often miraculous. After struggling with some excessive gabbiness recently, I decided it was time for another dose of Dale. With a renewed commitment to keeping my lips sealed and my ears open, several new opportunities came up, including:

- A $650,000 commitment from a new equity partner.

- A possible strategic alliance with a successful real estate investment group.

- Even more hugs and kisses from my daughters, who seem to be more consciously aware than anyone that I'm really paying attention to what they have to say.

One could argue that I would have gotten these same results with or without my mouth shut. But something deep down inside me says otherwise. And so does Dale Carnegie, who once said, "The ideas I stand for are not mine. I borrowed them from Socrates. I swiped them from Chesterfield. I stole them from Jesus. And I put them in a book. If you don't like their rules, whose would you use?"[1]

The lesson here is keep your mouth shut and listen to what the investor wants. There's no need to explain every single subtle nuance of your fix-and-flip business. As quickly as possible, find out:

- What kind of return on investment (ROI) they are looking for.

- How much money they can invest.

- How long they can invest the money.

By asking these questions, you'll quickly discover if the investor has the time and money required to get into a flip deal. Their answers will also reveal whether or not they want to be an equity or debt partner. For example, if the prospective investor tells you that they'd be content with a 10%–12%, you may suggest a lender/borrower arrangement.

Finally, and most importantly, through this Q&A process you'll learn if the investor is a PITA.

Tools of the Trade

The analytical investor will likely want to see financials for some or all of deals you've closed. I generally provide a basic Excel spreadsheet that includes:

---

[1] Interview, *Newsweek* (August 8, 1955).

- The date the property was purchased and sold

- Repair costs

- Holding costs

- Closing costs/commissions

- Pretax profit to the investor

I also use QuickBooks to keep a profit and loss statement for each property, as well as a balance sheet that lists my company's assets and liabilities. I highly recommend you take a class on both Excel and Quickbooks because eventually you'll meet a sophisticated investor that expects more thorough financial reporting.

Tip: Become an expert user in both Quickbooks and Excel. It'll help you keep track of your progress—and success—more easily. It'll also help you provide a clear window into your business that investors will appreciate.

Partnerships: Equity Partners

There are several ways to "paper up" an agreement with an equity partner. You can:

- Use a joint venture agreement.
- Create a limited liability company with operating agreement.
- File a Form D and create a private placement memorandum.

Let's look at each one in more depth.

Joint Venture Agreement

This is a basic legal document that specifies each party's responsibilities in the business arrangement. Let's say you find an investor with $100,000, and together you decide to purchase a distressed property to fix and flip. The joint venture agreement may state that you are in charge of finding the property, hiring the trades, scheduling the repairs, and listing the house for sale. The investor will agree to purchase the property, insure it, and pay the contractors on time. Any profit earned on the sale will be split equally.

It's important to note that a joint venture agreement is not a legal entity like a limited liability company or limited partnership. Therefore, the joint venture cannot own real property. You and the investor must determine who will go on title prior to acquisition. If the investor takes title in his or her name, then the proceeds must be distributed to you after the close of escrow.

Joint venture agreements are inexpensive to draft (seek an attorney, usually around $200–$500) and easy to execute. You won't need to keep a separate set of books or file a tax return for the joint venture either. However, the downside is security. If you agree to let the investor hold title and then he or she refuses to pay you when the deal closes, then you'll have to go to court to get your money.

LLC with Operating Agreement

A limited liability company with operating agreement is another way to structure an equity partnership. In the example I used above, you would act as the LLC's manager and the investor would be the member. The operating agreement would spell out how profit is distributed. As the manager, you'd have the same responsibilities as in the joint venture agreement. However, the investor may be more comfortable letting you maintain the books and hire the trades because he or she has an equitable interest in the property.

Both you and the investor can be comfortable knowing that the property is in an LLC you own together. Proceeds would be distributed from the company's checking account to you (the manager) and the investor (the member). In addition to maintaining a bank account the LLC would need to file a separate tax return at the end of the year. An attorney or accountant can set up an LLC for you for approximately $500–$1,000.

■ **Tip**:   Before you enter into an LLC with an investor, try a joint venture first just to make sure you are compatible.

Form D and Private Placement Memorandum

By filing a Form D with the SEC you can legally offer your investment opportunity to accredited investors. The SEC defines an accredited investor as

> . . . *a natural person who has individual net worth, or joint net worth with the person's spouse, that exceeds $1 million at the time of the purchase, excluding the value of the primary residence of such person or a natural person with income exceeding $200,000 in each of the two most recent years or joint income with a spouse exceeding $300,000*

for those years and a reasonable expectation of the same income level in the current year.[1]

However, even with accredited investors, you still are not allowed to do any general solicitation.

Most accredited investors will ask to see a *private placement memorandum* for the offering prior to investing. A PPM is the private equity version of a public investment prospectus. The PPM describes the opportunity and outlines the risks.

With the help of an attorney, I recently created a $500,000 private equity fund. A Form D was filed with the SEC, and each investor was provided the private placement memorandum. The fund is actually a limited partnership. Manny and I act as the general partners and the investors are limited partners. Each investor receives a return based on his or her capital contribution.

The upside is we can flip multiple properties at the same time. And if a deal goes bad there are others in the "pool" to offset the loss. The investor risk is reduced because of the volume of deals the fund can acquire, rehab, and sell for a profit.

The downside is that these are very expensive to set up. We spent over $10,000 creating the private placement memorandum and filing the Form D with the SEC.

■ **Tip:** Because private equity funds are so expensive to set up, don't bother unless you can pool at least $500,000 or so.

Seek Legal Advice Before Accepting Capital

Regardless of how you decide to enter into a business agreement with an investor, be sure to seek legal advise before accepting any funds. I also recommend you meet with a knowledgeable accountant who has real estate investment experience. There are serious tax and legal consequences if you fail to set up a partnership properly.

I can't tell you which type of arrangement will work best. You and your investor partner will need to decide on the design of the deal. If you plan to flip just one property together, then a joint venture agreement may be

---

[1] http://www.sec.gov/answers/accred.htm

sufficient. However, if you plan to do multiple deals with the same investor, I recommend an LLC. If you have several accredited investors that are comfortable "pooling" their money together, a private equity fund is likely your best option.

■ **Tip:** Again, don't go seeking investors without consulting an attorney about the dos and don'ts. A good attorney can also advise you on the best legal structure for the purpose at hand.

Private Money: Debt Partners

Debt partners (also known as private money or hard-money lenders) don't care about an equity position in your deal. All they want is a stable rate of return. And since the property you want to buy is distressed, don't expect to get a sweetheart interest rate from a private money lender. If you find a mom-and-pop lender, they'll probably want 8%–10% simple interest. The larger, more institutionalized lenders want 12%–18%.

Here's what else they'll likely require:

- A down payment of 20%–30% (or more)
- Monthly interest payments
- A loan origination fee
- Points (1–4) based on the loan size
- A personal guarantee

These lenders will also want to be in senior lien position in front of any junior lien holders. Most use a standard promissory note and deed of trust (or mortgage depending on what state you live in) to securitize the loan.

▧ **Note**: You're not going to find anyone to lend you money at a rate in the single digits unless you're really lucky (or it's your rich sister). Get used to it. The saving grace is that you're not using the money for that long.

Should You Pay Cash or Use Hard Money?

I had made up my mind. No more debt.

No more credit cards. No more car payments. No more hard-money loans.

Sure, paying 18% was steep. But that wasn't the real reason I decided to give up leveraging my fix-and-flip deals. Borrowing money had broken me after the market crashed in 2008. The funny thing about creditors is they don't care if your real estate investment portfolio drops in value by 65%—they still want their monthly payment.

Then the summer of 2009 rolled around. I owned two free-and-clear flip deals that were both in escrow to sell. I also had $45,000 in the bank. A wholesaler called me about a nice property he had just picked up at an auction.

The purchase price was $80,000 and the house needed about $5,000 in repairs. I knew in good condition it would sell for at least $115,000. Unfortunately, I didn't have enough cash to take the deal down. And, I had drawn a line in sand—no more hard-money loans.

But, the great thing about lines in the sand is that they're easy to erase.

This deal was too good to pass up, so I used hard money. 47 days later I sold the house and netted $18,000 in profit after paying a $900 loan origination fee and 18% interest to the lender.

I've been using hard money ever since. Here's why:

- With $100,000 cash and 75% leverage, I can buy three $80,000 houses and still have $40,000 left over for improvements and holding costs. After closing, I net $12,000 in profit for each property, a total of $36,000.

- With $100,000 cash and no leverage, I buy one $80,000 house, and have $20,000 left over for improvements and holding costs. After closing, I net $18,000 in profit.

Of course, using leverage can be risky, and costly.

However, tying up all your cash on one deal can carry an equal amount of risk. You could break even or, worse, lose money on that one deal. And while your cash is tied up in that one bad deal, several other great ones pass you by.

How to Find a Hard-Money Lender

Prior to the boom, hard-money lenders were in short supply. There was so much upside to flipping properties that few were willing to give up an equity position in a deal. Nowadays there's more security in lending. Here in Phoenix, I get two to three letters a week from private lenders offering 10%–18% with 0–4 points paid at closing. Search "hard money" on Google and you'll get pages full of results. A few of the larger lenders fund nationwide. If you've got a deal lined up at 20%–30% to put down, it shouldn't be difficult to find a trustworthy lender in your area.

When you find one, here's what they'll likely want from you:

- A loan application
- The property's address
- Estimate of repairs for the property
- Photos of the property (maybe)
- Proof of funds (maybe)
- Closing date
- Contact information for the title company or closing attorney

If you've done your due diligence, none of this should be an issue.

You'll want to make sure the lender you choose actually has the money to fund the deal and can close quickly. How do you find this out? Ask for some references or proof of funds. Losing a deal because the lender doesn't have the money is not good. It will cost you the earnest money deposit and a profitable deal.Hard-Money Lender

Equity vs. Debt Partners

I use a combination of equity and debt partners for most of my deals. I use the equity partner to fund the down payment, rehab, and holding costs. The debt partner covers 70-80% of the purchase price of the property. I profit share with the equity partner and pay interest to the debt partner. Here's what a typical deal looks like:

- $150,000—property purchase price
- $105,000—loan from debt partner (private money lender)
- $45,000—down payment (provided by the equity partner)

- $15,000—rehab and holding costs (provided by the equity partner)

The equity partner funds the deal through an unsecured promissory note to my company or through an LLC we create together. The debt partner loans the money to the LLC and secures it with a note and deed of trust in senior lien position. In this scenario, I have no money in the deal and I split any profits with the equity partner. However, I have total control throughout the acquisition, rehab, and sales phase of the transaction.

Why would an equity or debt partner give me all the control with absolutely no skin in the game? I have a successful track record of fixing and flipping houses. I've also lost money before, and when that happens I'm completely transparent. I provide updates and financial breakdowns for every deal so these partners trust me with their money.

If you plan to make fixing and flipping houses your full-time business, you'll eventually run out of your own money and need to use other peoples' money to fund acquisition and rehab. Combining equity and debt partnerships is a powerful way to grow your business exponentially. However, it requires careful bookkeeping and superior customer service skills. I have a fiduciary responsibility to my investors and I take my relationship with them very seriously. They are my clients. If they decide to invest elsewhere, I risk going out of business.

Tip: Whenever you're contemplating a loan to see a deal through, run the numbers carefully to ensure you're making money and not just spinning your wheels.

Conclusion

I have two offices. One is located in a modest single-level building in downtown Gilbert, Arizona. The other has four wheels and smells like breath mints (my daughter loves those things). Whether I'm at my desk or behind the wheel of my car, you can bet I'm listening to local sports radio.

Not long before I started writing this book, I was listening to my favorite station. In between talk of the Arizona Cardinals and the Phoenix Suns basketball team, I got clobbered over and over by an obnoxious commercial.

Yet another real estate investing guru was in town promoting his foreclosure boot camp. The ad was dripping with promises of investment secrets revealed, no money or credit required, flipping deals in 30 days or less, and huge profits with little effort required. Oh, and did I leave out that seating for this can't-miss-event was limited? Yuck.

I've been in the business for over ten years and have experienced massive success and colossal failure. Do you want to know what the secret to real estate investing success is? *There are no secrets.* No magic dust. No path of least resistance. No short cuts. However, there are a lot of painful truths, like:

- It takes money to buy real estate. (Maybe not your money, but somebody involved in the deal will need the cash to close and for you to get paid.)
- It takes time to buy real estate. (Good deals aren't growing on trees.)
- Most contractors overpromise and underdeliver.
- You will not get rich quick.
- You will have to work hard (nights and weekends included).

- Someone will take advantage of you, quite probably someone you trust.

- Someone may sue you or threaten to sue you.

- At some point you will lose money.

- The real estate investment guru is selling his program because he's broke and needs to raise money to start doing his own deals.

- Buyers are liars.

- Sellers are worse.

Real estate investing is a business. Most businesses take three to five years to become successful. So it's absurd to think that a one-day real estate investing training course will result in unthinkable profits. If it were that easy everyone would be a real estate investor.

▌**Note:** If you learn nothing more from this book, remember that there are no secrets to real investing. Everything you need to know you can learn through experience, reading books like this one, and talking with others in the business.

The Most Valuable Piece of Real Estate in the World

People say and do funny things at Christmas parties. Back in my days as a cameraman, I attended a company Christmas celebration at the Hard Rock Café in Phoenix. From across the room, I saw my new boss belly up to the bar and order a drink. Because I believe no one should ever drink alone I quickly made my way over to him. When I asked what he was sipping he proudly announced, "Scotch!" That's my favorite, I told him. He promptly ordered me a Glen-something and went on to educate me about the origins of the beverage. After 30 minutes of malt talk and a scarred esophagus from this nasty cocktail, I was sorely regretting my decision to suck up to the guy.

Then there was the time I ran into a title representative I know at a karaoke Christmas party a Realtor friend of mine hosts every year. After we exchanged the usual pleasantries, she asked me about my business. I told her I'd been taking some real estate investment classes—self-directed IRA, business financial management and tax strategy classes to be specific. She chuckled and told me that she would never need to take investment classes like these, because she's been in the title business for 15 years. She quickly added that she owned five rental properties. Really, I asked? Do you do straight-line depreciation on them or cost segregation? Her face went blank.

I've been a full-time real estate investor for more than ten years. During that time I've bought and sold more than 250 properties in Arizona, Texas, and Illinois. In a single month in 2006, I acquired 13 houses without a dime of my own money or credit. In 2009, I was accredited by the Arizona Department of Real Estate to teach a three-hour continuing education course for Realtors. I've appeared on local TV and radio discussing real estate investment strategies. And because of my experience, I was given the tremendous opportunity to write about real estate investing on BiggerPockets.com, an online community for real estate investors with over 100,000 members.

You would think with all of this education and experience a guy like me would have little use for continuing education. Not so. I regularly invest in the most valuable piece of real estate in the world: the six inches between my ears.

Since 2001, I've spent almost $30,000 and hundreds of hours in the classroom. The subject matter varied—from real estate technology to acquisition strategies to market analysis. It was time and money well spent. I learned how to turn my smart phone into a powerful real estate planning and marketing tool, how to calculate contract ratios for a specific neighborhood, and a better way to quickly analyze a property's value.

In *The Psychology of Selling: The Art of Closing the Sale*, Brian Tracy asks, "Would you hire an attorney that had no law books or see a doctor that hadn't had any ongoing training since leaving medical school?"[1] Of course not! So why should we real estate investors be any different? Real estate investing, like medicine, law, or accounting should be treated like a discipline. Continuing education is essential.

Where do you go to find it? Attend the next real estate investment club meeting in your area. Drop by a real estate school near you and pick up a catalog. Seek out successful real estate investors and ask them what classes they recommend.

As for my title rep friend at the Christmas party, she ended up having the last laugh. While she didn't know the difference between straight-line depreciation and cost segregation, at least she had enough common sense to stay away from the karaoke machine. I, on the other hand, decided to belt out "You're the One that I Want" from the *Grease* soundtrack.

---

[1] Brian Tracy, *The Psychology of Selling: The Art of Closing the Sale*. Nightingale-Conant. Out of print.

History had repeated itself. Once again I left a Christmas party with deep regret—and a sore throat.

■ **Tip:** Invest in yourself. And continue to invest in yourself throughout your career.

The Importance of a Mentor

As a boy, my interests were in sports, music, and movies. I had this rotating dream of being like Dan Fouts of the San Diego Chargers, Chris Cornell of Soundgarden, and Harrison Ford from the Indiana Jones films. How wonderful to be as wealthy and talented as these guys. But did I ever play football? Very little. What about learning the guitar and taking voice lessons? Of course not. As for acting? I never enrolled in a single drama class. These weren't real goals of mine; they were whims. Like most people, I just dreamt of being great.

Consequently, I spent all of my childhood and most of my adult years thinking that success came naturally to people. These gifted individuals didn't have to earn their success or have someone show them how to get it. A cosmic force had granted them special talents that I didn't deserve. I was left to toil away in mediocrity with the rest of the common folk.

Then it all changed in 1994 while working as a cameraman for KMGH in Denver, Colorado. For the first time in my professional life, I set a goal. It was to become the National Press Photographer Association Regional Photographer of the Year. I'm not exactly sure what prompted me to set this goal, but I was determined to reach it. I started spending hours at the TV station before and after my shift watching other photojournalists' reels. I immersed myself in the craft. I convinced some of the best in the business to mentor me. And within one year I had my trophy.

As I reflect on this accomplishment and the many others I've had since then, I can't help but wonder why it took me so long to discover that success is not preordained and certainly not a do-it-yourself proposition? History is ripe with stories of great men and women who attribute their success to a mentor or series of mentors. They didn't do it on their own; they had a lot of guidance.

Benjamin Graham mentored one of wealthiest investors of all time. Born in 1894, Graham lived through and actually prospered following the Great Depression. His book, *The Intelligent Investor*, was published in 1949 and inspired a generation of value investors. Mr. Graham's most successful protégé was so inspired by the book that he moved to New York from his modest, Midwestern hometown at the age of 20 to attend Columbia University.

Graham taught classes there at the time, in addition to managing his very successful investment firm, the Graham-Newman Corporation.

Graham's star pupil was named Warren Buffett. Buffett would later write in a revised edition of *The Intelligent Investor*, "I knew Ben as my teacher, my employer, and my friend. In each relationship—just as with all his students, employees and friends—was an absolutely open-ended, no-scores kept generosity of ideas, time and spirit. If clarity of thinking was required, there was no better place to go. And if encouragement or counsel was needed, Ben was there."[2]

So there you have it. If arguably the most successful business owner and investor of all time had a mentor, then shouldn't you and I? The truth is we are all born unsuccessful. As Earl Nightingale points out in *The Strangest Secret*, "Success is the progressive realization of a worthy goal or ideal."[3] We don't become successful until we set out on the journey to make our goal a reality. For me it was to win an award. After I left the television industry, it was to build a successful real estate investment business. For Warren Buffett, it was to become a millionaire by age 35.

The journey can be very cold and lonely without help. So set your goal and then immediately begin to surround yourself with people who can help you achieve it. Good luck!

Never forget: If you really want to succeed in your fix-and-flip business, you will. Period.

---

[2] Benjamin Graham, *The Intelligent Investor*. Collins Business, 2003.

[3] Earl Nightingale, *The Strangest Secret*. Wilder Publications, 2011 (reprint).

Appendices

In the appendices that follow, you will find:

- Appendix A: Scope of Work Agreement

- Appendix B: Independent Contractor Agreement

- Appendix C: Deed of Trust

- Appendix D: Promissory Note

- Appendix E: Sample HUD Settlement Statement (HUD-1)

- Appendix F: IRS Form W-9 (page 1 only)

In your work as a fix and flipper, you will need such documents on a regular basis. Please note that these are for illustration only—they may not work in your situation or in your state or locality. You should always have a reputable local lawyer set you up with similar documents and review agreements before you sign them.

Scope of Work

PROJECT

SCOPE OF WORK

This document serves as a Scope of Work (SOW) to the Independent Contractor Agreement dated as of November 20, 2012 (herein the "Agreement"), by and between EXAMPLE COMPANY, LLC (herein "COMPANY") and EXAMPLE CONTRACTOR, LLC (herein "Contractor"), which is hereby incorporated by reference.

Description of Services.

Location. Contractor agrees to perform all required contracting Services relating to the rehabilitation ("rehab") of real property owned by COMPANY located at 123 Main Street, Phoenix, AZ 85123 (herein the "Project").

Method of Performing Services. Contractor will determine the method, details, and means of completing the Project. Contractor agrees to devote the required personnel for a minimum of forty (40) hours per week to the Project.

Tools and Instrumentalities. Contractor, at its own expense, will supply all tools, instrumentalities and all building and installation materials for the Project, including without limitation paint, sheetrock, tape, mud, framing materials, insulation, patching materials, Durock, green-board, Drylock, mortar spacers, decking boards and cleaning supplies.

Finishing Materials. COMPANY shall be responsible for procuring the finishing materials as provided herein.

Work Items:

Exterior Work

- Prep and Paint Finish of Entire House, including:

  - Caulk exterior surfaces as necessary, prime all bare wood

  - Paint stucco, trim, doors, soffits, fascia, using 3-color paint scheme

Interior Work

- Paint Entire Interior (Ceilings, Wall, Trim) Using 3-Color Paint Scheme

- Replace all lighting/fan fixtures, including:

  - Replace (4) Fan/Light Combos

  - Replace (10) Interior/Exterior Light Fixtures

  - Install Appliances (Refrigerator, Stove, Microwave, Dishwasher, Washer, Dryer)

Compensation.

In consideration for the Services to be performed by Contractor, COMPANY agrees to pay Contractor the sum of THREE THOUSAND TWO HUNDRED SIXTY DOLLARS ($3,260.00), to be paid based on the following payment schedule:

$800.00 upon signing of this contract;

$1000.00 upon substantial completion of all Exterior Work;

$1000.00 upon substantial completion of all Interior Work;

$460.00 upon completion of specified Punch List items;

Deadline.

Contractor agrees to substantially complete the Project no later than November 24, 2012. For each additional full week past this deadline, Contractor shall pay COMPANY a two-hundred dollar ($200.00) fee, to be deducted from the final payment from COMPANY. Contractor agrees and acknowledges that such payment is not meant to penalize Contractor, but is a reasonable estimation of the damages COMPANY will suffer due to such delay. No penalty shall be assessed if the delay is due to COMPANY's mis-scheduling of contractors.

Expenses.

COMPANY will not reimburse Consultant for any out-of-pocket expenses incurred in connection with the Project.

Term.

This SOW will become effective on the date first written above, and will continue in effect until all the Project has been completed and paid for, or until this SOW is terminated by means set forth in the Agreement.

EXAMPLE COMPANY, LLC

By:_____

Your Name Here, Your Title Here

EXAMPLE CONTRACTOR, LLC

By:_____

Contractor Name, Title

Independent Contractor Agreement

Independent Contractor Agreement

This Independent Contractor Agreement (this "Agreement") is made as of November 20th, 2012, by and between EXAMPLE COMPANY, LLC, a Arizona limited liability company (herein "COMPANY"), and EXAMPLE CONTRACTOR, LLC, a Arizona limited liability company with its principal office address at 555 First Street, Phoenix, Arizona 85123 (herein "Contractor").

For valuable consideration, the receipt and adequacy of which are hereby acknowledged, the parties hereto agree as follows:

1. **Services.** COMPANY may retain Contractor in connection with COMPANY's real property improvements to one or more of COMPANY's properties. If COMPANY retains Contractor, then Contractor will provide the construction/general contractor services (herein the "Services") described in any Scope of Work (herein a "SOW"). The initial SOW is attached hereto as Exhibit A and incorporated herein by reference. The location of the Services will be set out in the applicable SOW. Contractor may retain, at Contractor's own discretion and expense, such

employees and/or subcontractors as Contractor deems necessary to perform the Services.

2. **Compensation.** COMPANY will compensate Contractor in consideration for the Services by paying the fees described in the applicable SOW.

3. **Term and Termination.** This Agreement shall be effective for a period of one (1) year starting on the date hereof and will renew automatically for successive one (1) year terms unless terminated as prescribed herein. COMPANY may terminate this Agreement or any SOW for any reason, on at least seven (7) days' prior written notice, which notice shall specify the exact date of termination. Either party may terminate this Agreement or any SOW for cause immediately upon written notice.

4. **Representations and Warranties.** Contractor represents and warrants that:

   (a) it is a corporation or limited liability company, duly incorporated or organized, validly existing, and in good standing under the laws of the State of Georgia:

   (b) its Federal Employer Identification Number is ____-_____;

   (c) it has and will maintain all insurance required by law and Section 10 of this Agreement;

   (d) its personnel are legally authorized to work in the United States in accordance with all applicable immigration laws;

   (e) it currently has multiple clients/customers, has had multiple clients/customers in the past, and intends to have multiple clients/customers in the future;

   (f) it makes its services available to the general public and does not make its services exclusively available to COMPANY;

   (g) it will maintain accurate financial records in connection with the performance of this Agreement and any SOW and the conduct of its business;

   (h) it will comply with all applicable laws and is not prohibited from performing its obligations under this Agreement or any SOW by any other agreement; and

(j) it will provide the Services in a workmanlike manner consistent with industry standards.

5. **Indemnification.** Contractor agrees to indemnify, hold harmless, and defend COMPANY from and against any and all judgments, liabilities, damages, losses, expenses, and costs (including without limitation court costs and reasonable attorney's fees) incurred by COMPANY which relate to: (i) Contractor's willful misconduct or negligence in connection with this Agreement or any SOW; (ii) Contractor's breach of any representation, warranty, or obligation under this Agreement or any SOW; (iii) the violation of any licensure or bond requirement; and (iv) Workers' Compensation claims, overtime claims, tax liability claims, benefits claims, or other liabilities imposed against COMPANY by Contractor's employees or any other party (including governmental bodies and courts), whether relating to Contractor's status as an independent contractor or the status of its personnel.

6. **Non-Disclosure.** To the extent applicable, Contractor will protect and keep confidential all non-public information disclosed by COMPANY (herein "Confidential Information"), and will not, except as may be authorized by COMPANY in writing, use or disclose any such Confidential Information for any purpose other than the performance of this Agreement and any SOW. Upon expiration or termination of this Agreement or any applicable SOW, Contractor will return to COMPANY all written materials that contain any Confidential Information.

7. **Non-Solicitation.** During the term of this Agreement and for a period of one (1) year thereafter, Contractor will not solicit or hire any employee or independent contractor of COMPANY with which Contractor had contact in connection with this Agreement or any SOW.

8. **Independent Contractor Status.**

(a) The parties hereto are independent contractors. Nothing herein shall be deemed to create any form of partnership, principal-agent relationship, employer-employee relationship, or joint venture between the parties hereto. Contractor will provide the Services using its own independent skill and judgment.

(b) COMPANY will have no right or responsibility hereunder to provide instructions or training, require any work other than what is agreed to by Contractor in this Agreement or any SOW, choose or supervise the personnel used to perform the Services, set Contractor's hours or location of work, other than the actual construction site when required, set the order for or sequence of performing the Services, require progress reports, or provide tools, facilities or equipment.

9. **Acknowledgment.** Contractor hereby acknowledges and agrees that:

(a) neither Contractor nor any of its employees is an employee of COMPANY;

(b) neither Contractor nor any of its employees is entitled to any benefits provided or rights granted by COMPANY to their respective employees, including without limitation group insurance, liability insurance, disability insurance, retirement plans, health plans and the like;

(c) COMPANY will not make any deductions on behalf of Contractor for any U.S. federal or state taxes or FICA taxes;

(d) COMPANY will not have any obligation to provide Worker's Compensation coverage for Contractor or to make any premium overtime payments at any rate other than the normal rate agreed to in writing by COMPANY, if applicable;

(e) it will be Contractor's sole responsibility to provide Worker's Compensation and pay any premium overtime rate, for its employees who provide Services under this Agreement or any SOW and to make required FICA, income tax withholding, and other payments, including compensation for Services, related to such employees; and

(f) Contractor will provide COMPANY with suitable evidence of Contractor's compliance with this Section 9 whenever requested.

10. **Insurance.** Contractor, at its own expense, will obtain for itself and its personnel Worker's Compensation insurance in statutory amounts. Contractor will also obtain Commercial General Liability insurance with limits of liability of not less than one million dollars ($1,000,000.00) naming COMPANY as an additional insured. Contractor will provide a certificate to COMPANY of such insurance coverage upon request.

11. **Limitation of Liability.** IN NO EVENT WILL COMPANY HAVE ANY LIABILITY OR RESPONSIBILITY FOR ANY INDIRECT, INCIDENTAL, EXEMPLARY, SPECIAL OR CONSEQUENTIAL DAMAGES, EVEN IF ADVISED OF THE POSSIBILITY OF SUCH DAMAGES.

12. **Injunctive Relief.** Contractor acknowledges and agrees that money damages would be an inadequate remedy for any breach or threatened breach of any of the provisions of this Agreement or any SOW. Accordingly, in addition to any other relief available to it, COMPANY will be entitled to specific performance and other appropriate injunctive and equitable relief with respect to any such breach or threatened breach. Further, it is agreed that in the event of a single occurrence of breach of this Agreement or any SOW by Contractor, it would be impracticable or extremely difficult to determine the actual damages incurred by COMPANY, and, therefore, Contractor shall pay to COMPANY as liquidated damages, and not as a penalty, the amount of two thousand dollars ($2,000.00).

13. **Arbitration.** Any controversy between the parties hereto involving the construction or application of any of the terms, covenants, or conditions of this Agreement or any SOW will, upon the written request of one party served on the other, be submitted first to informal mediation and then to arbitration. The parties will each appoint one person to hear and attempt to informally resolve the dispute, and, if they are unable to do so, then the two persons shall select a third person who shall act as the impartial arbitrator whose decision shall be final. The arbitration shall comply with and be governed by the Commercial Rules of the American Arbitration Association. The cost of arbitration will be borne in such proportions as the arbitrator decides. Judgment upon the award rendered by the arbitrator may be entered in any court of competent jurisdiction.

14. **Assignment.** Contractor may not assign or subcontract its rights or obligations under this Agreement or any SOW without

the prior written consent of COMPANY. Any unauthorized assignment shall be null and void.

15. **Waiver.** Neither party will be deemed to have waived any provision hereof unless such waiver is in writing and executed by a duly authorized officer of the waiving party. No waiver by either party of any provision hereof will constitute a waiver of such provision on any other occasion.

16. **Severability.** The invalidity or unenforceability, in whole or in part, of any provision, term, or condition hereof will not affect the validity or enforceability of the remainder of such provision, term or condition or of any other provision, term, or condition.

17. **Notices.** All notices and other communications in connection with this Agreement or any SOW shall be in writing and shall be deemed to have been received by a party three (3) days after mailing, registered or certified, postage prepaid with return receipt requested, to each party's principal office address. Notices delivered personally shall be deemed communicated as of the date of actual receipt. Either party may change its notice address upon written notice to the other party.

18. **Governing Law.** This Agreement and all SOWs will be governed by and is construed in accordance with the internal laws of the State of Georgia without regard to its rules concerning conflicts of law provisions. Each party agrees to the exclusive venue and jurisdiction of the state/superior courts situated in Cobb County, Georgia or, in the case of federal jurisdiction, federal courts situated in Fulton County, Georgia.

19. **Entire Agreement.** This Agreement and all SOWs constitute the entire agreement between COMPANY and Contractor and specifically supersede any previous Independent Contractor's Agreements dated prior to November 20, 2012. In the event that any provisions in any SOW are in conflict with the provisions in this Agreement, then the provisions in this Agreement will prevail over any such conflicting provisions. This Agreement may not be amended unless such amendment is in writing and signed by both parties hereto.

IN WITNESS WHEREOF, the parties have caused this Agreement to be executed by their respective duly authorized officers as of the date set forth above.

EXAMPLE COMPANY, LLC

By:_____

Your Name Here, Your Title Here

EXAMPLE CONTRACTOR, LLC

By:_____

Contractor Name, Title

Deed of Trust and Assignment of Rents

When recorded mail to:

=addressee=

Deed of Trust and Assignment of Rents

Date:

TRUSTOR: _____

whose mailing address is: _____

TRUSTEE: _____

whose mailing address is: _____

BENEFICIARY: _____

whose mailing address is: _____

Property situate in the County of _____, State of Arizona, as described as follows:

Together with all buildings, improvements and fixtures thereon or hereinafter erected thereon.

Street address if any, or identifiable location of this property:

_____

THIS DEED OF TRUST, made on the above date by, between and among the TRUSTOR, TRUSTEE and BENEFICIARY above named.

WITNESSETH: That Trustor hereby irrevocably grants, conveys, transfers and assigns to the Trustee in Trust, with Power of Sale, the above described real property (the Trust Property), together with leases, issues, profits, or income therefrom (all of which are hereinafter called "property income"): SUBJECT, however, to the right, power and authority hereinafter given to and conferred upon Beneficiary to collect and apply such property income:

SUBJECT TO: Current taxes and other assessments, reservations in patents and all easements, rights of way, encumbrances, liens, covenants, conditions, restrictions, obligations, and liabilities as may appear of record.

For the Purpose of Securing:

A. Payment of the indebtedness in the principal sum of $_____ evidenced by a Promissory Note or Notes of even date herewith, and any extension or renewal thereof, executed by Trustor in favor of Beneficiary or order.

B. Payment of additional sums and interest thereon which may hereafter be loaned to Trustor, or his successors or assigns, when evidenced by a Promissory Note or Notes reciting that they are secured by a Deed of Trust.

C. Performance of each agreement of Trustor herein contained.

To Protect the Security of This Deed of Trust, Trustor Agrees:

1. To keep said property in good condition and repair; not to remove or demolish any building thereon; to complete or restore promptly and in good and workmanlike manner any building which may be constructed, damaged, or destroyed thereon, and to pay when due all claims for labor performed and materials furnished therefore; to comply with all laws affecting said property or requiring any alterations or improvements to be made thereon; not to commit or permit waste thereof; not to commit, suffer, or permit any act upon said property in violations of law; and do all other acts which from the character or use of said property may be reasonably necessary, the specific enumerations herein not excluding the general.

2. To provide, maintain, and deliver to Beneficiary fire insurance satisfactory to and with loss payable to Beneficiary. The amount collected under any fire or other insurance policy may be applied by Beneficiary upon any indebtedness secured hereby and in such order as Beneficiary may determine, or at option of Beneficiary the entire amount so collected or any part thereof may be released to Trustor. Such application or release shall not cure or waive any default or notice of Trustee's sale hereunder or invalidate any act done pursuant to such notice.

3. To appear in and defend any action or proceeding purporting to affect the security hereof or the rights or powers of Beneficiary or Trustee; and to pay all costs and expenses of Beneficiary and Trustee, including cost of evidence of title and attorney's fees in a reasonable sum, in any such action or proceeding in which Beneficiary or Trustee may appear or be named, and in any suit brought by Beneficiary or Trustee to foreclose this Deed of Trust.

4. To pay, before delinquent, all taxes and assessments affecting said property; when due, all encumbrances, charges, and liens, with interest, on said property or any part thereof, which appear to be prior or superior hereto; all costs, fees, and expenses of this Trust, including, without limiting the generality of the foregoing, the fees of Trustee for issuance of any Deed of Partial Release and Partial Reconveyance or Deed of Release and Full Reconveyance, and all lawful charges, costs, and expenses in the

event of reinstatement of, following default in, this Deed of Trust or the obligations secured hereby.

Should Trustor fail to make any payment or to do any act as herein provided, then Beneficiary or Trustee, but without obligation so to do and without notice to or demand upon Trustor and without releasing Trustor from any obligation hereof, may make or do the same in such manner and to such extent as either may deem necessary to protect the security hereof. Beneficiary or Trustee being authorized to enter upon said property for such purposes; appear in and defend any action or proceeding purporting to affect the security hereof or the rights or powers of Beneficiary or Trustee; pay, purchase, contest, or compromise any encumbrance, charge, or lien which in the judgment of either appears to be prior or superior hereto; and, in exercising any such powers, pay necessary expenses, employ counsel, and pay his reasonable fees.

5. To pay immediately and without demand all sums expended by Beneficiary or Trustee pursuant to the provisions hereof, together with interest from date of expenditure at the same rate as is provided for in the note or notes secured by this Deed of Trust or at the legal rate if it secures a contract or contracts other than a promissory note or notes. Any amounts so paid by Beneficiary or Trustee shall become a part of the debt secured by this Deed of Trust and a lien on said premises or immediately due and payable at option of Beneficiary or Trustee.

It Is Mutually Agreed:

6. That any award of damages in connection with any condemnation or any such taking, or for injury to the property by reason of public use, or for damages for private trespass or injury thereto, is assigned and shall be paid to Beneficiary as further security for all obligations secured hereby (reserving unto the Trustor, however, the right to sue therefore and the ownership thereof subject to this Deed of Trust), and upon receipt of such moneys Beneficiary may hold the same as such further security, or apply or release the same in the same manner and with the same effect as above provided for disposition of proceeds of fire or other insurance.

7. That time is of the essence of this Deed of Trust, and that by accepting payment of any sum secured hereby after its due date, Beneficiary does not waive his right either to require prompt

payment when due of all other sums so secured or to declare default for failure so to pay.

8. That at any time or from time to time, and without notice, upon written request of Beneficiary and presentation of this Deed of Trust and said note(s) for endorsement, and without liability therefor, and without affecting the personal liability of any person for payment of the indebtedness secured hereby, and without affecting the security hereof for the full amount secured hereby on all property remaining subject hereto, and without the necessity that any sum representing the value or any portion thereof of the property affected by the Trustee's action be credited on the indebtedness, the Trustee may: (a) release and reconvey all or any part of said property; (b) consent to the making and recording, or either, of any map or plat of the property or any part thereof; (c) join in granting any easement thereon; (d) join in or consent to any extension agreement or any agreement subordinating the lien, encumbrance, or charge hereof.

9. That upon written request of Beneficiary stating that all sums secured hereby have been paid, and upon surrender of this Deed of Trust and said note(s) to Trustee for cancellation, and upon payment of its fees, Trustee shall release and reconvey, without covenant or warranty, expressed or implied, the property then held hereunder. The recitals in such reconveyance of any matters or facts shall be conclusive proof of the truthfulness thereof. The grantee in such reconveyance may be described as "the person or persons legally entitled thereto."

10. That as additional security, Trustor hereby gives to and confers upon Beneficiary the right, power, and authority, during the continuance of this Trust, to collect the property income, reserving to Trustor the right, prior to any default by Trustor in payment of any indebtedness secured hereby or in performance of any agreement hereunder, to collect and retain such property income as it becomes due and payable. Upon any such default, Beneficiary may at any time, without notice, either in person, by agent, or by a receiver to be appointed by a court, and without regard to the adequacy of any security for the indebtedness hereby secured, enter upon and take possession of said property or any part thereof, in his own name sue for or otherwise collect such property income, including that past due and unpaid, and apply the same, less costs and expenses of operation and

collection, including reasonable attorney's fees, upon any indebtedness secured hereby, and in such order as Beneficiary may determine. The entering upon and taking possession of said property, the collection of such property income, and the application thereof as aforesaid, shall not cure or waive any default or notice of Trustee's sale hereunder or invalidate any act done pursuant to such notice

11. That upon default by Trustor in the payment of any indebtedness secured hereby or in performance of any agreement hereunder, Beneficiary may declare all sums secured hereby immediately due and payable by delivery to Trustee of written notice thereof, setting forth the nature thereof, and of election to cause to be sold said property under this Deed of Trust. Beneficiary also shall deposit with Trustee this Deed of Trust, said note(s), and all documents evidencing expenditures secured hereby.

Trustee shall record and give notice of Trustee's sale in the manner required by law, and after the lapse of such time as may then be required by law, subject to the statutory rights of reinstatement, the Trustee shall sell, in the manner required by law, said property at public auction at the time and place fixed by it in said notice of Trustee's sale to the highest bidder for cash in lawful money of the United States, payable at time of sale. Trustee may postpone or continue the sale by giving notice of postponement or continuance by public declaration at the time and place last appointed for the sale. Trustee shall deliver to such purchaser its Deed conveying the property so sold, but without any covenant or warranty, expressed or implied. Any persons, including Trustor, Trustee, or Beneficiary, may purchase at such sale.

After deducting all costs, fees, and expenses of Trustee and of this Trust, including cost of evidence of title in connection with sale and reasonable attorney's fees, Trustee shall apply the proceeds of sale to payment of all sums then secured hereby and all other sums due under the terms hereof, with accrued interest; and the remainder, if any, to the person or persons legally entitled thereto, or as provided in A.R.S. 33-812. To the extent permitted by law, an action may be maintained by Beneficiary to recover a deficiency judgment for any balance due hereunder.

In lieu of sale pursuant to the power of sale conferred hereby, this Deed of Trust may be foreclosed in the same manner provided by law for the foreclosure of mortgages on real property. Beneficiary shall also have all other rights and remedies available him hereunder and at law or in equity. All rights and remedies shall be cumulative.

12. That Beneficiary may appoint a successor Trustee in the manner prescribed by law. A successor Trustee herein shall, without conveyance from the predecessor Trustee, succeed to all the predecessor's title, estate, rights, powers, and duties. Trustee may resign by mailing or delivering notice thereof to Beneficiary and Trustor, by registered or certified mail, and by recordation of a Notice of Resignation of Trustee in the office of the County Recorder in each County in which trust property or some part thereof is situated.

13. That this Deed of Trust applies to, inures to the benefit of, and binds all parties hereto, their heirs, legatees, devisees, administrators, executors, successors, and assigns. The term Beneficiary shall mean the owner and holder of the note(s) secured hereby, whether or not named as Beneficiary herein. In this Deed of Trust, whenever the context so requires, the masculine gender includes the feminine and neuter, and the singular number includes the plural.

14. That Trustee accepts this Trust when this Deed of Trust, duly executed and acknowledged, is made a public record as provided by law. Trustee is not obligated to notify any party hereto of pending sale under any other Deed of Trust or of any action or proceeding in which Trustor, Beneficiary, or Trustee shall be a party unless brought by Trustee.

15. The Note secured by Deed of Trust created herein shall become immediately due and payable in full upon the sale, assignment or transfer of any of the Trustor's right, title or interest in and to the subject property.

The undersigned Trustor requests that a copy of any notice of Trustee's sale hereunder be mailed to him at his address hereinbefore set forth.

TRUSTOR

_____

(Trustor's Name)

STATE OF ARIZONA } ss On _____, 20__ before me, the undersigned Notary
County of Maricopa   Public, personally appeared _____ ,
                           personally known to me (or proved to me on the basis
                           of satisfactory evidence) to be the person(s) whose
                           name(s) is/are subscribed to the within instrument.
                           WITNESS my hand and official seal.

                           _____

                           Notary Public
                           My commission will expire: _____

Promissory Note

Promissory Note

Principal amount: $_____ Date: _____

For value received, the undersigned, EXAMPLE, LLC, an Arizona limited liability company (the "Maker"), hereby promises to pay to the order of _____ (the "Holder") the sum of _____ and no/100 dollars of the United States of America (U.S. $_____.00) (the "Principal"), together with simple interest accrued thereon at the rate of twelve (12%) percent per annum on the unpaid balance (the "Interest") pursuant to this Promissory Note (the "Note").

The Principal and Interest shall be paid to the Holder in the following manner at the following address:

[Address for payments to Holder]:

_____.

Any and all payments shall be first applied to accrued and unpaid Interest and the balance to Principal. This Note may be prepaid, at any time, in whole or in part, without penalty. Prepayment of a partial amount of Principal shall result in a re-calculation of the total amount due according to this Note. Notwithstanding the promise to pay the Interest as described herein, the Maker agrees to pay an amount in addition to the Interest (the "Participation Payment") according to an agreement with the Holder to participate in profits derived from the sale of certain real property (the "Participation Agreement"), which agreement is attached hereto and incorporated herein by reference.

The Principal and accrued Interest shall be due and payable from the Maker to the Holder, in full on the ___ day of _____, 201_ (the "Maturity Date"), provided however, if the Holder is entitled to a Participation Payment, then the Maturity Date shall be established as of the date of the closing of the sale of the real property identified in the Participation Agreement.

This Note shall at the option of the Holder thereof be immediately due and payable upon the occurrence of any of the following: (1) Failure of Maker to make any payment due hereunder within ten (10) days of its due date; (2) Upon the dissolution or liquidation of the undersigned Maker; (3) Upon the filing by Maker of an assignment for the benefit of creditors, bankruptcy or other form of insolvency or by suffering an involuntary petition in bankruptcy or receivership not vacated within thirty (30) days.

In the event this Note shall be in default and placed for collection, then the undersigned Maker agrees to pay all reasonable attorney fees and costs of collection. Any payments not made within ten (10) days of due date shall not be subject to a late charge. All payments hereunder shall be made to the address above or to such address as may from time to time be designated in writing by the Holder.

The undersigned Maker agrees to remain fully bound until this Note shall be fully paid and waives demand, presentment and protest and dishonor, and further agrees to remain bound, notwithstanding any protest and all notices hereto and, notwithstanding any extension, modification, waiver, or other indulgence or discharge or release of any obligation hereunder. No modification or indulgence by the Holder hereof shall be binding unless in writing signed by the Holder; and any indulgence on any one occasion shall not be an indulgence for any other or future occasion. The rights of the Holder hereof shall be cumulative and not necessarily successive. This Note be construed, governed and enforced in accordance with the laws of the State of Arizona.

In Witness Whereof, the Maker executes this Promissory Note as of the date above written.

EXAMPLE, LLC [Maker]

By: _____

    Manager

Sample HUD Settlement Statement

OMB Approval No. 2502-0265

A. **Settlement Statement (HUD-1)**

B. Type of Loan					
1. ☐ FHA 2. ☐ RHS 3. ☐ Conv. Unins.	6. File Number:	7. Loan Number:	8. Mortgage Insurance Case Number:		
4. ☐ VA 5. ☐ Conv. Ins.					

C. Note: This form is furnished to give you a statement of actual settlement costs. Amounts paid to and by the settlement agent are shown. Items marked "(p.o.c.)" were paid outside the closing; they are shown here for informational purposes and are not included in the totals.

D. Name & Address of Borrower:	E. Name & Address of Seller:	F. Name & Address of Lender:
G. Property Location:	H. Settlement Agent:	I. Settlement Date:
	Place of Settlement:	

J. Summary of Borrower's Transaction		K. Summary of Seller's Transaction	
100. Gross Amount Due from Borrower		**400. Gross Amount Due to Seller**	
101. Contract sales price		401. Contract sales price	
102. Personal property		402. Personal property	
103. Settlement charges to borrower (line 1400)		403.	
104.		404.	
105.		405.	
Adjustment for items paid by seller in advance		**Adjustment for items paid by seller in advance**	
106. City/town taxes to		406. City/town taxes to	
107. County taxes to		407. County taxes to	
108. Assessments to		408. Assessments to	
109.		409.	
110.		410.	
111.		411.	
112.		412.	
120. Gross Amount Due from Borrower		**420. Gross Amount Due to Seller**	
200. Amount Paid by or in Behalf of Borrower		**500. Reductions in Amount Due to Seller**	
201. Deposit or earnest money		501. Excess deposit (see instructions)	
202. Principal amount of new loan(s)		502. Settlement charges to seller (line 1400)	
203. Existing loan(s) taken subject to		503. Existing loan(s) taken subject to	
204.		504. Payoff of first mortgage loan	
205.		505. Payoff of second mortgage loan	
206.		506.	
207.		507.	
208.		508.	
209.		509.	
Adjustments for items unpaid by seller		**Adjustments for items unpaid by seller**	
210. City/town taxes to		510. City/town taxes to	
211. County taxes to		511. County taxes to	
212. Assessments to		512. Assessments to	
213.		513.	
214.		514.	
215.		515.	
216.		516.	
217.		517.	
218.		518.	
219.		519.	
220. Total Paid by/for Borrower		**520. Total Reduction Amount Due Seller**	
300. Cash at Settlement from/to Borrower		**600. Cash at Settlement to/from Seller**	
301. Gross amount due from borrower (line 120)		601. Gross amount due to seller (line 420)	
302. Less amounts paid by/for borrower (line 220)	( )	602. Less reductions in amounts due seller (line 520)	( )
303. Cash ☐ From ☐ To Borrower		**603. Cash** ☐ To ☐ From Seller	

The Public Reporting Burden for this collection of information is estimated at 35 minutes per response for collecting, reviewing, and reporting the data. This agency may not collect this information, and you are not required to complete this form, unless it displays a currently valid OMB control number. No confidentiality is assured; this disclosure is mandatory. This is designed to provide the parties to a RESPA covered transaction with information during the settlement process.

L. Settlement Charges

700. Total Real Estate Broker Fees		Paid From Borrower's Funds at Settlement	Paid From Seller's Funds at Settlement
Division of commission (line 700) as follows :			
701. $ to			
702. $ to			
703. Commission paid at settlement			
704.			

800. Items Payable in Connection with Loan			
801. Our origination charge	$	(from GFE #1)	
802. Your credit or charge (points) for the specific interest rate chosen	$	(from GFE #2)	
803. Your adjusted origination charges		(from GFE #A)	
804. Appraisal fee to		(from GFE #3)	
805. Credit report to		(from GFE #3)	
806. Tax service to		(from GFE #3)	
807. Flood certification to		(from GFE #3)	
808.			
809.			
810.			
811.			

900. Items Required by Lender to be Paid in Advance			
901. Daily interest charges from to @ $ /day		(from GFE #10)	
902. Mortgage insurance premium for months to		(from GFE #3)	
903. Homeowner's insurance for years to		(from GFE #11)	
904.			

1000. Reserves Deposited with Lender				
1001. Initial deposit for your escrow account		(from GFE #9)		
1002. Homeowner's insurance	months @ $	per month $		
1003. Mortgage insurance	months @ $	per month $		
1004. Property Taxes	months @ $	per month $		
1005.	months @ $	per month $		
1006.	months @ $	per month $		
1007. Aggregate Adjustment		-$		

1100. Title Charges			
1101. Title services and lender's title insurance		(from GFE #4)	
1102. Settlement or closing fee	$		
1103. Owner's title insurance		(from GFE #5)	
1104. Lender's title insurance	$		
1105. Lender's title policy limit $			
1106. Owner's title policy limit $			
1107. Agent's portion of the total title insurance premium to	$		
1108. Underwriter's portion of the total title insurance premium to	$		
1109.			
1110.			
1111.			

1200. Government Recording and Transfer Charges			
1201. Government recording charges		(from GFE #7)	
1202. Deed $ Mortgage $ Release $			
1203. Transfer taxes		(from GFE #8)	
1204. City/County tax/stamps Deed $ Mortgage $			
1205. State tax/stamps Deed $ Mortgage $			
1206.			

1300. Additional Settlement Charges			
1301. Required services that you can shop for		(from GFE #6)	
1302.	$		
1303.	$		
1304.			
1305.			

1400. Total Settlement Charges (enter on lines 103, Section J and 502, Section K)			

Comparison of Good Faith Estimate (GFE) and HUD-1 Charges		Good Faith Estimate	HUD-1
Charges That Cannot Increase	**HUD-1 Line Number**		
Our origination charges	# 801		
Your credit or charge (points) for the specific interest rate chosen	# 802		
Your adjusted origination charges	# 803		
Transfer taxes	# 1203		

Charges That In Total Cannot Increase More Than 10%		Good Faith Estimate	HUD-1
Government recording charges	# 1201		
	#		
	#		
	#		
	#		
	#		
	#		
	#		
	Total		
	Increase between GFE and HUD-1 Charges	$ or	%

Charges That Can Change		Good Faith Estimate	HUD-1
Initial deposit for your escrow account	# 1001		
Daily interest charges $ /day	# 901		
Homeowner's insurance	# 903		
	#		
	#		
	#		

Loan Terms

Your initial loan amount is	$
Your loan term is	years
Your initial interest rate is	%
Your initial monthly amount owed for principal, interest, and any mortgage insurance is	$ includes ☐ Principal ☐ Interest ☐ Mortgage Insurance
Can your interest rate rise?	☐ No ☐ Yes, it can rise to a maximum of %. The first change will be on and can change again every after . Every change date, your interest rate can increase or decrease by %. Over the life of the loan, your interest rate is guaranteed to never be lower than % or **higher** than %.
Even if you make payments on time, can your loan balance rise?	☐ No ☐ Yes, it can rise to a maximum of $
Even if you make payments on time, can your monthly amount owed for principal, interest, and mortgage insurance rise?	☐ No ☐ Yes, the first increase can be on and the monthly amount owed can rise to $. The maximum it can ever rise to is $
Does your loan have a prepayment penalty?	☐ No ☐ Yes, your maximum prepayment penalty is $
Does your loan have a balloon payment?	☐ No ☐ Yes, you have a balloon payment of $ due in years on
Total monthly amount owed including escrow account payments	☐ You do not have a monthly escrow payment for items, such as property taxes and homeowner's insurance. You must pay these items directly yourself. ☐ You have an additional monthly escrow payment of $ that results in a total initial monthly amount owed of $. This includes principal, interest, any mortgage insurance and any items checked below: ☐ Property taxes ☐ Homeowner's insurance ☐ Flood Insurance ☐ ☐ ☐

Note: If you have any questions about the Settlement Charges and Loan Terms listed on this form, please contact your lender.

IRS Form W-9

| Form **W-9**
(Rev. December 2011)
Department of the Treasury
Internal Revenue Service | **Request for Taxpayer
Identification Number and Certification** | **Give Form to the
requester. Do not
send to the IRS.** |

Print or type — See Specific Instructions on page 2.

Name (as shown on your income tax return)

Business name/disregarded entity name, if different from above

Check appropriate box for federal tax classification:
- ☐ Individual/sole proprietor
- ☐ C Corporation
- ☐ S Corporation
- ☐ Partnership
- ☐ Trust/estate

☐ Limited liability company. Enter the tax classification (C=C corporation, S=S corporation, P=partnership) ▶ _____

☐ Other (see instructions) ▶

☐ Exempt payee

Address (number, street, and apt. or suite no.)

Requester's name and address (optional)

City, state, and ZIP code

List account number(s) here (optional)

Part I   Taxpayer Identification Number (TIN)

Enter your TIN in the appropriate box. The TIN provided must match the name given on the "Name" line to avoid backup withholding. For individuals, this is your social security number (SSN). However, for a resident alien, sole proprietor, or disregarded entity, see the Part I instructions on page 3. For other entities, it is your employer identification number (EIN). If you do not have a number, see *How to get a TIN* on page 3.

Note. If the account is in more than one name, see the chart on page 4 for guidelines on whose number to enter.

Social security number

| | | | – | | | – | | | | |

Employer identification number

| | | – | | | | | | |

Part II   Certification

Under penalties of perjury, I certify that:

1. The number shown on this form is my correct taxpayer identification number (or I am waiting for a number to be issued to me), and

2. I am not subject to backup withholding because: (a) I am exempt from backup withholding, or (b) I have not been notified by the Internal Revenue Service (IRS) that I am subject to backup withholding as a result of a failure to report all interest or dividends, or (c) the IRS has notified me that I am no longer subject to backup withholding, and

3. I am a U.S. citizen or other U.S. person (defined below).

Certification instructions. You must cross out item 2 above if you have been notified by the IRS that you are currently subject to backup withholding because you have failed to report all interest and dividends on your tax return. For real estate transactions, item 2 does not apply. For mortgage interest paid, acquisition or abandonment of secured property, cancellation of debt, contributions to an individual retirement arrangement (IRA), and generally, payments other than interest and dividends, you are not required to sign the certification, but you must provide your correct TIN. See the instructions on page 4.

Sign Here   Signature of U.S. person ▶   Date ▶

General Instructions

Section references are to the Internal Revenue Code unless otherwise noted.

Purpose of Form

A person who is required to file an information return with the IRS must obtain your correct taxpayer identification number (TIN) to report, for example, income paid to you, real estate transactions, mortgage interest you paid, acquisition or abandonment of secured property, cancellation of debt, or contributions you made to an IRA.

Use Form W-9 only if you are a U.S. person (including a resident alien), to provide your correct TIN to the person requesting it (the requester) and, when applicable, to:

1. Certify that the TIN you are giving is correct (or you are waiting for a number to be issued),

2. Certify that you are not subject to backup withholding, or

3. Claim exemption from backup withholding if you are a U.S. exempt payee. If applicable, you are also certifying that as a U.S. person, your allocable share of any partnership income from a U.S. trade or business is not subject to the withholding tax on foreign partners' share of effectively connected income.

Note. If a requester gives you a form other than Form W-9 to request your TIN, you must use the requester's form if it is substantially similar to this Form W-9.

Definition of a U.S. person. For federal tax purposes, you are considered a U.S. person if you are:

- An individual who is a U.S. citizen or U.S. resident alien,

- A partnership, corporation, company, or association created or organized in the United States or under the laws of the United States,

- An estate (other than a foreign estate), or

- A domestic trust (as defined in Regulations section 301.7701-7).

Special rules for partnerships. Partnerships that conduct a trade or business in the United States are generally required to pay a withholding tax on any foreign partners' share of income from such business. Further, in certain cases where a Form W-9 has not been received, a partnership is required to presume that a partner is a foreign person, and pay the withholding tax. Therefore, if you are a U.S. person that is a partner in a partnership conducting a trade or business in the United States, provide Form W-9 to the partnership to establish your U.S. status and avoid withholding on your share of partnership income.

Cat. No. 10231X   Form **W-9** (Rev. 12-2011)

Index